SEEKING
SOULMATE

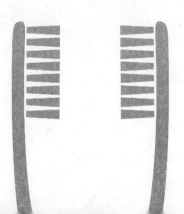

Parallax Press
P.O. Box 7355
Berkeley, CA 94707
parallax.org

Parallax Press is the publishing division of
Unified Buddhist Church, Inc.
© 2017 Chamin Ajjan
All rights reserved
Printed in the United States of America

Cover and text design by John Barnett | 4eyesdesign.com
Author photograph © Mangue Banzima
Cover illustration © Shutterstock
Printed on 100% post-consumer waste recycled paper

Library of Congress Cataloging-in-Publication Data is available.

1 2 3 4 / 20 19 18 17

SEEKING SOULMATE

Ditch the
Dating Game
and Find Real
Connection

Chamin Ajjan
MS, LCSW, ACT

PARALLAX PRESS

BERKELEY, CALIFORNIA

CONTENTS

INTRODUCTION

Remember when you were a kid dreaming about your first date? Who would it be with? Where would you go? What would your first kiss be like? Would your parents allow you to date? It was all so exciting! However, that excitement changes for many of us when we get older. As awkwardness, insecurity, and societal pressures creep in, dating can become a ritual we have to engage in, a means to an end, a burden, and a chore. The glamorous dating world portrayed on television and in the movies is not exactly what is happening in real life.

When online dating became a thing, I was right there with my friends helping them with their profiles. I relished their stories, but started to see that I was having more fun *hearing* about them than my friends were having actually *living* through them. At the same time, I noticed that the single clients in my psychotherapy practice were experiencing a similar level of disappointment and distress in their dating experiences. It became very clear to me that dating was not fun for many people. In fact, it was the number one complaint my single clients discussed in session. The problem solver and behavioral specialist in me realized this was a fairly common human issue that needed more attention.

Seeking Soulmate started as a small workshop I created called the Mindful Dating Workshop, which focused on all of the dating issues that my single clients in New York City seemed to complain about. They felt frustrated, weary, disillusioned, and hopeless about the dating process. Finding a decent partner seemed impossible because dating was too difficult to navigate. All of my clients were great potential partners, but they internalized what they perceived as dating failure to be their fault, a sign that they were meant to be alone, or an indication that there were no eligible suitors out there. So I decided to create a space where we could discuss these difficulties, focus on our perceptions, learn new tools, explore what is within our control, let go of negativity, and practice self-care.

The workshop was so successful that I decided to blog about the principles of Mindful Dating so that a wider audience could learn how apply them. Then, out of nowhere, many years later I received an email from a book editor who had discovered my blog and thought it would make a great book. Jennifer Kamenetz encouraged me to write a book proposal and submit it to Parallax Press, the publishing company where she worked. You should have seen my face when I got off of the phone with her and told my husband that an editor wanted me to write an entire book about mindful dating. A book! Yeah, I had thought about writing a book, but had not entertained my idea as more than a fantasy. And who gets an email from a publisher asking them to submit a proposal? I felt like I was being "punked!" After laughing about it a bit and discussing it with my husband, I realized I had nothing to lose for trying. And thus a book was born. Thanks, Jen!

There are so many books out there about dating. How could I make mine different? How could I make it relevant? And how could I keep readers engaged? Doubt crept in. However, once I really got started, I realized that I did not have to worry about any of those things. I have a wealth of insight and information that I owe to the many wonderful single clients I have worked with over the years. I have a unique perspective as a therapist that I can offer along with solid clinical advice.

In my pursuit to make this book a genuine reflection of me as a clinician and a real honest-to-goodness human being, I use both personal and professional experiences. That means you will be hearing about client interactions and clinical observations in addition to my own personal blunders, successes, interactions, and influences. How can I ask you to be your authentic self if I am not doing the same? Opening up and making myself vulnerable in this book was liberating and scary at the same. I hope to give you a true sense of who I am as a psychotherapist, mother, wife, daughter, black woman, pop culture junkie, perpetual student, and more.

For all of these reasons, *Seeking Soulmate* may not read like other dating books. Think of me as your girlfriend who just happens to be a therapist. We are two friends chatting about the dating world and I am sharing what I have learned. This book is not meant to be a how-to book. I am not arrogant enough to believe that there is only one way of approaching dating. I do not think there is a concrete set of rules to follow that will result in your finding the partner of your dreams. I definitely do not believe that there is only one way to catch a partner. If that book existed, then there would not be the need for any other books to follow it. We are unique individuals who bring our own distinct experiences to the table. A "one size fits all" approach does not apply to dating.

My clients often tell me that I make Cognitive Behavioral Therapy (CBT) seem approachable and understandable. It is important to me to share what I know about CBT and do so in way that is applicable—and hopefully fun. The combination of CBT principles and mindfulness principles you'll find in this book do just that. Years of training with many skilled clinicians and practice have given me the foundation to present these evidence-based clinical models in a new and appealing way.

Change is inherently challenging, so it is important that we do not lose ourselves, get frustrated, and burn out as we make changes. It is my hope that you will enjoy learning these new skills and be kind to yourself as you grow and sometimes stumble and fall, but always get back up and stay on course.

This book is not about how you can be completed by a relationship. That scene in the movie *Jerry McGuire* where Tom Cruise tells Renee Zellweger, "You complete me," is so romantic and iconic. It is also total crap! No relationship will complete you. You complete yourself. A relationship should not be about filling some hole you feel you have in your life. It should be about enriching it. Looking to someone else to fill a void in your life will only end in resentment and disaster. That applies to having children as well, but that is another book....

Simply reading this book is not intended to magically transform your dating life. Real change can come from this book, but only if you dedicate yourself to practicing the principles outlined in it. And that will take time. I want for you to have realistic expectations as you begin to read. Some things may click immediately while others may take time to sink in. Mindfulness is a journey with no final destination. That means you will be learning a new way of paying attention to the world that will be strengthened and become more developed with a lifelong practice. This book may or may not be your first time learning about mindfulness. However, it should certainly not be your last. Continue learning new ways to be mindful and keep up the practice for continued results in all parts of your life.

Seeking Soulmate is meant to be a guide. I want for you to use it as a friendly dating resource that will remind you of what is important to stay aware of. I want the book to serve to inspire you with a different approach you can take while dating, which can lead you to have a more peaceful and enjoyable experience. I intend for the book to help you identify your true authentic self, making it more possible for you to feel complete on your own. I want you to learn to respond to your negative thoughts so that you can be more present as you date. And I want you to change any unhelpful behavioral patterns that may be interfering with your chances of finding true happiness. If you can do that, then you can open up a whole new world of opportunities, creating more possibility for you to make a genuine connection with a potential partner.

Thank you for taking this journey with me. Enjoy the ride!

Top Ten Dating Myths

Before you even start dating you may begin to receive messages from family, peers, books, television and the general media about what to expect when you date. This advice is often well intended but not completely accurate. I hope this book will help you to have a new outlook on dating and disprove some of the myths that have impacted the way you date. This Top Ten list highlights some of the more common myths to reevaluate.

1. If you have sex too early, they'll never call you again.

2. Men are more likely than women to approach someone they are interested in.

3. Sparks will fly immediately if there is something there.

4. If it is not love at first sight then you should just give up.

5. Opposites attract.

6. When you stop looking for a relationship, that is when you will find someone.

7. There is a better half out there for you.

8. What your friends and family think of your relationship is not important.

9. Love conquers all.

10. If they love you, they will change.

PART ONE
WHAT IS MINDFUL DATING?

1 MIND, BODY, FEELINGS, AND BEHAVIOR

Picture this: Gigi, a beautiful, successful woman, gets into her dream car after spending a fun evening with her girlfriends and drives to her beautiful condo. She enters her apartment feeling sad and lonely. She thinks, *I wish I had a boyfriend to come home to like my friends do. There must be something wrong with me. I'm never going to find a partner.* She longs for a relationship, and after years of looking for "the one," the mere idea of dating leaves her feeling anxious and hopeless. It seems so easy for some of her friends. She feels like a failure—a loser. She feels undesirable and un-dateable. She is on an online dating service and has a date for tomorrow night with a guy who seems to be a good match ... but so have all of the others. And they all turned out to be losers, jerks, opportunists, players, or guys who are only interested in getting laid and not in developing a meaningful relationship.

Gigi already knows the date tomorrow is going to be a waste of time. She has the thought, *Online dating never works out!* Her feelings of sadness and hopelessness increase. *What's the point of putting myself through that again?* she asks herself. The next night, Gigi stands her date up. Her anxiety and sadness decrease momentarily ... but in the long run she has a much more negative outlook on dating—and the very thought of it makes her worry.

Many women find dating stressful—even though we have been told it is meant to be fun and exciting. Not every woman struggles in the same way as Gigi ... however, many can relate to her feelings of hopelessness and anxiety—and to her critical thoughts. When talking about why dating can be so hard, we can come up with a whole truckload of reasons. *There are not enough eligible guys, the ones who are available suck, I'm not trying hard enough, I'm not attractive enough, I'm too intimidating, I don't know how to act on a date, the only guys who like me are losers,* etc. If any of these reasons sound familiar, it means dating is causing you distress. That distress can lead you to act in ways that sabotage your dating life. You might avoid dating altogether. Or you might go into new dates making negative predications that come true. Some may even question why they want to be in a relationship so badly, and they criticize themselves because of it. In my psychotherapy practice, people often report rejecting a potential mate before he can reject them (even if they are totally into him). These kinds of thoughts and behaviors lead to more dating distress and a less successful dating experience.

Are you ready to break out a pint of Chunky Monkey ice cream and drown your sorrows yet? Well hold off, because there is a solution. Mindful dating can help make the process a lot less stressful and more enjoyable. It addresses the negative thoughts, self-destructive behaviors, and lack of awareness that we all find ourselves experiencing from time to time, and it provides you with useful tools to be able to manage these problems. It can also help you have an authentic dating experience and open up the possibilities of a true love connection.

Since the beginning of time we have had interest in the sport of love, dating, courting, and mating. Any chance Adam and Eve would have been just as interesting to us if they were only homies? Not likely. There are countless romantic novels that explore the woes and the triumphs of the subject. Cultural practices have been built around it. Tales have been told and retold of the classic, inspirational, and often tragic love of such iconic couples as Marc Antony and Cleopatra or Bonnie and Clyde. It is why there has been so much success with dating shows like *The Dating Game, The Love Connection,* and *Singled Out.* We have even ventured into reality TV shows like *The Bachelor/Bachelorette* franchise, *Finding*

Prince Charming—and my guilty pleasure, *Dating Naked*. In these shows we delight in the awkward and sometimes painful experiences of folks looking for their happily ever after.

Why are we so fascinated with dating? Well, the truth is that everybody wants to experience love and companionship. Even the most independent person who seems to have it all feels a sense of longing for an intimate connection. That is because as human beings we have a natural capacity to love and to be loved. Connecting with others and cultivating deep and lasting relationships are instinctive to our species. We need each other. These lessons are both innate and taught. We learn from a very young age that life and happiness can be summed up by that popular playground song where two lovers meet sitting in a tree, "K-I-S-S-I-N-G." But what is the message we are receiving from this song, love stories, our cultural practices, and from television, movies, and the media? Often the message is that dating and love are simple and should not take work. That it should happen naturally—and if that is not true for you, then you must be doing it wrong. This simplistic view can create negative thoughts, sadness, and downright frustration about yourself and your abilities to find your "soulmate."

" ... this idealistic belief that love should be simple and easy is way too absolute."

Now, it is true that finding love can be easier for some more than others. However, this idealistic belief that love should be simple and easy is way too absolute. We all have things we need to work on to be in a happy, healthy, and long-lasting relationship. If you don't have things to work on, then you are in a small minority, and you are reading the wrong book! For the rest of us, the work may be about learning how to be more social and more confident—or letting go of the five-piece matching DVF baggage set that we have been hauling around with us. You may have trust issues that make it difficult to fully commit to any intimate relationship. Others may have no problem finding a partner. In fact, they continue to find the same unhealthy relationship over and over and over again in a different form with different people.

There are a ton of reasons why dating may be hard for you. Mindful dating helps you identify these reasons and then manage them more effectively.

What is mindful dating? Before we talk about it, let me explain more about mindfulness and my love affair with it. I was born in Hollywood and raised in West Hollywood, where mindfulness has always seemed to be present in some form in my life. I can remember my mother doing simple yoga poses as a child, seeing my friends' parents meditate, and being exposed to yoga in elementary school. In the past thirty years, mainstream mindfulness has spread across the country and has gained in popularity. Recently it has even become trendy, being given the celebrity seal of approval from the likes of Eva Mendes, Angelina Jolie, Hugh Jackman, and even Oprah! Switching to the East Coast, you cannot walk a block in Brooklyn today without spotting a yoga studio or a meditation space. Mindfulness may seem to have popped up out of nowhere, but in fact, people have been practicing mindfulness for thousands of years.

Mindfulness has its origins in Buddhism, and its practice has been scientifically proven to be an effective approach to healing physical and mental ailments. It spread through the Western world when mindfulness meditation teacher, clinical researcher, pioneer, and icon, Jon Kabat-Zinn, created his successful Mindfulness-Based Stress Reduction program—which then inspired the rock stars of mindfulness, Zindel Segal, Mark Williams, and John Teasdal, to develop a new psychological treatment model, Mindfulness-Based Cognitive Therapy (MBCT). MBCT incorporates the principles of Cognitive Behavioral Therapy (CBT) and mindfulness practices. CBT in simple terms is all about how thoughts affect the way you feel, feelings affect the way you behave, behaviors affect the way you think—and vice versa. They are all interconnected. CBT has long been known to be one of the more effective evidence-based treatment models in psychotherapy. By marrying the two theoretical frameworks, a powerful new way to address the mind, body, and spirit became available to us, giving us the best of both worlds. I use both CBT and MBCT in my practice and have seen first-hand how useful mindfulness can be for those who suffer from depression, anxiety, and chronic pain—as well as for people who do not have a formal diagnosis but struggle with common life issues such as transitioning, work stress, partner discord, and yes, dating!

According to Kabat-Zinn: "Mindfulness means paying attention in a particular way; on purpose, in the present moment, and nonjudgmentally." You do this by cultivating awareness and learning to accept what is. If you are anything like me though, this concept is a challenge. It was a while before I could stop trying to control and change every little thing that I was unhappy with. I had to get in tune with the beliefs and thoughts that were driving my actions.

Mindfulness develops when you practice intentionally focusing on the present moment and on interacting with your environment in a way that allows things to be just as they are—without you trying to control, change or manipulate anything. But most of us are far from being mindfulness masters. In fact, I think we can all agree that there is a lot of mind-*less* behavior out there that causes a lot of problems for us. That is because in today's world we are constantly being pushed and pulled in so many directions. Our workdays are longer. We can be overscheduled with friends and family. Smartphones have become a staple that we cannot seem to function without. "Multitasking" has become the norm, and balancing all of our responsibilities has left us unable to truly be in the moment and pay attention to one task at a time. Recently I woke up at 6:30 a.m., got ready for work, replied to four emails, made breakfast for my daughter, threw her hair into a quick ponytail, walked out the house, choked down a banana, got to the subway at 7:15 a.m. ... and had no memory of how I got there. Is it because I suffer from dementia? I hope not! I think the more realistic answer is that my fast-paced morning rivaled the dazzling acrobatics of Cirque Du Soleil, and my attention was so split that I was unable to focus on one thing. Autopilot has become a way of life for many of us. When we navigate through life reflexively, we are not fully engaging in what we are doing. If we are not fully engaged in what we are doing, how can we make good choices for ourselves?

When Gigi arrived home after spending time with her friends, she felt sadness and loneliness almost immediately. That is because she had the thought, *I wish I had a boyfriend to come home to, like my friends do. There must be something wrong with me. I'm never going to find a partner.* If Gigi was more aware of her thinking, she could have responded to her thoughts. Perhaps she would have realized that she was predicting the future without having any real evidence she was going to die alone. Or maybe she would have seen how unfairly critical and hard she was being on herself. Instead, she was focused on what will or will not be, made negative predictions, and felt even worse.

"Mindfulness is all about being in the present moment instead of being stuck in the past or focused on the future."

Mindfulness is all about being in the present moment instead of being stuck in the past or focused on the future. By cultivating awareness of what is happening in the here and now, you give yourself the chance to fully participate in your life, instead of being reactive. Mindful dating is the practice of bringing awareness and other principles of mindfulness to your romantic encounters—and using them to remain present and open to yourself and a potential partner. I don't know how many times I have been in session with someone who was complaining about a date they went on and only had stories about themselves on the date. Yes, some superficial details about the other person might be shared, but mostly I hear about the negative feelings and thoughts my client was having. Sometimes my clients cannot even recall what they were talking about on the date. I believe this is because they are too busy focusing on themselves and are too stuck in their thoughts. Isn't dating about meeting someone new and seeing if there is a connection? It seems to me that you would have difficulty connecting with a date if you are not paying attention to them!

Another problem I see often is having unrealistic expectations. We bring so many expectations with us on a date. For example, "He should be this," "She must look a certain way," or "I have to feel that instant connection." These expectations, along with our negative past dating experiences, can lead to missing out on a wonderful relationship, falling for one that is not worth your time, or not even getting yourself into the game. Learning to date mindfully teaches you to pay attention to your expectations and how to respond to them.

One of the reasons why Gigi is so convinced that she will never find a partner is that she has been on countless bad dates—and believes in her bad track record when it comes to dating. She is determined not to get into another relationship with a self-centered, arrogant, and callous man again. So when she goes out with a guy for the first time, she is like a dating ninja, moving from one question to another to determine whether he fits this profile. As she works in her covert operation to sniff out the details of her suitor, she is also concealing her true identity, which prevents her from making a true connection. If Gigi were more open to her date and aware of her fears of falling for "another jerk," she could get a more genuine sense of her date and how she was feeling with him.

Through mindful dating you learn to be your true self and make a genuine connection. In other words, the more you learn to be present and in tune with your needs, the less focused you will be on trying to be what "they" want you to be—or what you want them to be.

THOUGHTS

Worries, ideas, scenarios, predictions, opinions, judgments, and beliefs are types of thoughts. These thoughts are occurring all of the time—even when you want to shut your mind off. I am all too familiar with lying in bed at night, dog-tired, while my mind keeps me awake with each of the problems I have to solve. But we are often unaware of what those individual thoughts are. To practice mindful dating, you must become more acquainted with your thoughts and your behaviors. Our minds are constantly at work. It is estimated that we have 50,000 to 70,000 thoughts per day. Yet we are often unconscious of them. Quick, tell me ten thoughts you had yesterday. Not so easy, is it? And I am just asking for a measly 0.01 percent of your thoughts! Imagine all of the other unrecognized thoughts you have that impact the choices you make.

As you get more familiar with how your mind works, you will start to see how your thoughts influence your behaviors and your mood. It is this very awareness that can lead to gaining control of your thoughts—as opposed to being controlled by them. Kabat-Zinn says mindfulness allows us to "see our thoughts as mental events that come and go in the mind like clouds across the sky instead of taking them literally. The idea that we're no good, unlovable, and ineffectual can finally be seen as just that—an idea—and not necessarily as the truth, which just might make it easier to disregard." In other words, thoughts are not facts! This is such a simple concept, but for many of us, negative thoughts are so compelling that we accept them as the truth. The same is true for our negative thoughts about dating. Twisted thinking around dating is normal when you have had several disappointing experiences. Those experiences leave wounds, and it is only human nature to protect yourself from harm. However, these wounds can create cognitive distortions—and if left unexamined, these twisted thoughts can become habitual. It then becomes more likely that you will have an automatic thought or make a snap judgment based on these warped ideas. By learning to objectively witness your thoughts about dating, you can prevent old habits that are favored by automatic pilot from ending a potential relationship before it has had a chance to develop.

"It is estimated that we have 50,000 to 70,000 thoughts per day."

We have already established that thoughts influence feelings, feelings influence behaviors, and behaviors influence thoughts. If we were to make visual representation of this idea, it would look like a perfect equilateral triangle where thoughts, feelings, and behaviors are respectively at one point of the triangle. When looking at the triangle, you can see how interconnected they are. You cannot change one side without there being an impact on the others. Now, you cannot directly change feelings. For example, I can't just say to myself, "Chamin, stop feeling jealous of Beyoncé's beauty, talent, fame, and fortune," and hope that the feeling will disappear. That is no more effective than you telling yourself to stop feeling sad or hopeless about dating. Frankly, it is a great way to set yourself up for failure. It can't be done! However, you can intervene by making changes to the way you are thinking and to your actions. So I can't stop my feelings of jealousy, but I can stop watching the "Drunk In Love" or "Lemonade" videos over and over again while comparing her flawless body to mine. I can recognize that the action of repeatedly watching the videos leads me to compare myself to Beyoncé and then to criticize myself with thoughts like, *She is perfect. I will never measure up to her,* or, *I wish I had her body.* I can restore a healthier sense of self by having compassion for myself and by remembering what I like about me; I can begin to let go of those feelings of jealousy. Similarly, you cannot stop feelings of insecurity, anxiety, or hopelessness from occurring on a date. However, you can learn to respond to the corresponding thoughts that are causing or influencing those feelings or intervene when you become aware of any behaviors that are impacting how you feel. You can do so in a kind and caring way, which can indirectly change how you are feeling in the moment.

Let's examine this further.

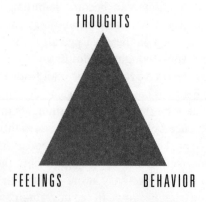

THOUGHTS

FEELINGS   BEHAVIOR

Our minds are always at work. As a result, we may not even realize what is actually going on in there. Without this knowledge, it can seem as if events themselves are causing our reactions. But that could not be farther from the truth. It is our interpretations of events that impact our emotional and behavioral reactions to situations. Imagine two people walking down a crowded street together on a beautiful sunny day. A hot red sports car with the top down, full of attractive yet rowdy guys, drives by and one of the guys yells out "Ugly!" Person A thinks, *Who does that? That guy has some serious issues,* and soon forgets about the incident. Person B thinks, *OMG! I am so humiliated. I knew I should have put on more make-up today. Everybody is looking at me now. I am ugly!* She begins to feel down and becomes withdrawn. Person A is able to move past the incident easily because she did not personalize it. In her mind, the guy could have been talking to anybody on the street or just looking for attention. It was not about her. Person B is deeply affected by the occurrence, internalizes the comment to be about her, validates it with her own negative beliefs about being unattractive ... and her mood changes. Both women were in the same place at the same time but experienced very different reactions.

It is not uncommon to believe that a situation itself is the cause of a reaction. Gigi made the assumption that dating will make her feel bad, so she cancelled the date. She jumped from the situation (dating) to the outcome (avoidance) and believed that dating was the cause of her reaction. However, it was her thoughts about dating being pointless and her predictions about her date being a loser that made her feel hopeless. In fact, these are the thoughts that often come to mind for Gigi when it comes to dating. They are called "automatic thoughts" because they pop into your mind automatically. Kind of like that annoying commercial jingle or pop tune you can't get out of your head. The tricky thing about automatic thoughts, and thoughts in general, is that they can seem so convincing and so compelling that you take them for truths. They are seductive, familiar, and somehow attractive, even though they are not good for you. They are the Cheese Whiz of the psyche. However, as I said before: Thoughts are not facts. They are just ideas. They may be true, but they may not be true. And that means they need to be fact-checked. Without being challenged, these automatic thoughts can become more and more ingrained into how we think about ourselves and the world around us. As you become more acquainted with your thoughts, you will start to understand how certain thoughts can lead to specific feelings.

We will learn more about how to do this later on. In the meantime, start to become more curious about your thoughts—and try to do so with the knowledge that they are just that ... thoughts, not facts.

FEELINGS

Many of us have a difficult time putting a finger on how we are feeling. We are given many confusing messages about feelings throughout our lives. Has anyone ever told you, "Don't be sad," or "Don't cry," in an effort to make you feel better? That person may have had great intentions, but the message we get from comments like these is that it is not okay to feel sad. You might think crying is bad or sign of weakness. Or that you must stop feeling sad right now. This is false. Crying, sadness, and other undesirable emotions have gotten a bad rap. They are normal and natural reactions to triggering events. They are not a sign of weakness or inherently a "bad" thing. All feelings are valid and have a purpose.

The alternative to feeling negative emotions is to deny your feelings, push them to the side, and ignore them. You know, like when the cool kids were coming over, and as they arrived you noticed your Hanson "MMMBop" single was on your desk, and you quickly kicked it under the bed never to be found again. However, this is not an effective coping strategy with feelings. Why? Because you cannot get rid of your feelings. They are simply stored away to later manifest in some unwanted, uncontrollable, and/or undesirable way. Trying to control feelings is like trying to stop a leak in a dam with a pebble. You might be able to stop the leak in the short term, but eventually that pebble is going to become dislodged by the rapid force of the river ... and the dam will break. The reality is that it takes strength to sit with uncomfortable feelings and to allow yourself to process them instead of ignoring them. Feelings will pass if you let them. Mindfulness can teach you how to sit with your uncomfortable or unwanted feelings.

Often there is confusion about the difference between a thought and a feeling. It is not unusual for me to ask a client how they are feeling and get a response like, "I feel like I am no good," or "I feel fed up with dating." Although those answers do give me some insight into what the patient is experiencing, they are thoughts—not feelings. With further questioning I might find that the emotions the patient was feeling were hopelessness, guilt, or sadness. This very small distinction can give you a big insight into yourself in the present moment. Learning to name your feelings is essential to being able to sit and be with them. Once you are able to identify and sit with your feelings, you will begin to be less reactive to them, get off autopilot, and start making active choices about how to behave.

"All feelings are valid and have a purpose."

BEHAVIOR

Behavior is what we do and how we do it. Our actions are influenced by our environments and our past experiences, and we adjust accordingly. There are some situations in which we respond to our environment reflexively—such as when the doctor hits our knee with a hammer and we automatically kick. However, for the most part, our behavior is voluntary. The good news is this means that change is possible and that there is something you can do about maladaptive behaviors that are getting you nowhere. The bad news is you are going to have to remove the words "I can't" from your vocabulary.

Dating can seem scary, dangerous, or threatening to many. It makes sense that you would protect yourself from possible danger. It is a human instinct to do so. It just comes naturally. If a rhinoceros is chasing me, you can believe

Fight-or-flight response: an automatic instinctual physiological response to a perceived danger.

I am getting the hell out of the way! Our brains are wired to react in this way. It is called the fight-or-flight response, and it is automatic. Our sympathetic nervous system responds to acute stress by activating hormones that result in preparation to deal with the threat. Basically, your body prepares to stand its ground and fight the threat—or to flee. However, the brain is not able to tell the difference between whether a fear is based in reality or simply a manifestation of your thinking. This means that goodnight kiss you have been obsessively worrying about for the entire date can be seen as such a big threat that you are unable to recognize that your thinking is distorted, and instead you interpret the imagined danger to be real. You really like this guy, and you have convinced yourself that a bad kiss will ruin your chances. As a result you give your date an awkward kiss that leaves you both dissatisfied and gives him the wrong signal.

With more awareness, you can learn to recognize whether a worry is real or imagined. This skill allows you to make a choice about how you will respond to that worry. Your behavior can go from being automatic and reactive to responsive and adaptive. When you learn to respond to situations, you have the ability to engage with them in a way that feels good and productive. You can feel more in control of yourself and less confused about why things didn't turn out the way you wanted them to. You will free up a lot of time because you will be engaged in fewer conversations with yourself about why you acted a certain way—or about how things got so out of control.

YOUR BODY

The body holds the answers to a lot of the questions you may have about your feelings and thoughts. The way we think about our bodies can have an impact on our emotions and subsequent behaviors. You may have been aware of this. But were you also aware that the condition of our bodies can also have an impact on our minds? Our bodies send messages to our brain about the state we are in, and our minds interpret these messages accordingly. One great illustration of this idea is something I like to call "smile therapy." I often assign homework to my clients with depression to be focused on smiling throughout the day. They can choose when and where to do this, but I like to suggest doing it while walking down the street because it makes the assignment interactive with your environment. This feels awkward to many people initially. Smiling when you are not feeling happy can seem inauthentic. But when this behavioral experiment is attempted with an open mind, the results can be surprising. Eventually, people notice an actual change in their mood. The sadness lifts a bit, and the smile on their face feels more genuine. This happens because their body is signaling to their mind that they are happy, and their mind follows suit.

"The body holds the answers to a lot of the questions you may have about your feelings and thoughts."

Body posture, aches and pains, facial expression, tension, and upset stomachs are a few examples of how your body can send information about how you are feeling and what you are thinking. However, most of us are so stuck in our minds that we are not paying attention to this vital information. If we cultivate more awareness of what our bodies are communicating to our minds then we can respond to those messages instead of being led by them. This gives us another entry point to manage discomfort around dating. Imagine waiting for a blind date to arrive. You may be feeling nervous or awkward. Butterflies or an upset stomach can accompany this feeling. As a result, you hunch over and tension builds in your shoulders. Your date finally shows up, but you are unable to truly engage with them. Your mind may interpret this information to mean that you are uncomfortable with your date, and this makes it even more difficult to interact. The nervous feeling becomes so strong that you end the date early. The date was over before it ever had a chance! If you were more mindful you could have acknowledged that blind dates are awkward for everyone (including your date). You could have responded to the tension in your shoulders by sitting up with your shoulders back. You could have called a friend for some quick moral support and to slap some sense back into you while you waited. Each one of these options could have changed how you were feeling and made it possible for you to actually enjoy your date.

We can see how our bodies send messages to our minds—and how that can impact the way we interact with our environment. But what about the thoughts we have about our bodies? How do these thoughts influence how we feel and behave? Our bodies can be a source of shame or pride. If you happen to be one of the people who suffer from poor body image, you are not alone. We are programmed in our society to uphold a very narrow standard of beauty that excludes the majority of us. It's as if we were told by society that we could only eat cheddar cheese and every other cheese was not good enough to be considered. No gruyere, no gouda, no parmesan, and no jarlsberg? As if! But our standard of beauty is just as limited. It is not fair, but it is reality. Heck, even the most revered supermodel, who exemplifies that narrow standard of beauty, can be hit by a wave of insecurity and self-doubt. We get these messages about what is considered to be beautiful constantly in print, on TV, at the movies, in store windows, at the dentist's office, etc. This content naturally leads us to compare ourselves to these images and this can result in poor body image.

Women are more prone to have a negative body image—and even the kids are doing it! Girls as young as ten years old worry about being fat. By the time they get to middle school, many of our girls are dissatisfied with multiple parts of their bodies. As we age and are confronted by younger and younger images of what beauty is, we can feel dissatisfied by our aging bodies—and as if our value in society has decreased because we are not represented. I have caught myself walking past a newsstand, seeing racy pictures of beautiful women displaying their round bottoms, and feeling shame about my "uncharacteristically flat" rump. Adolescent memories of my younger brother's friends teasing me about not having the acceptable butt of my black ancestors come to mind. This can have an impact on my body language, and my behavior may change. Instead of being my usual outgoing self, I may become more avoidant and isolate myself. In this example thoughts, feelings, behaviors, and body all converge and affect my sense of self and the way I interact with my environment.

We tend to be overly judgmental of our bodies. When we criticize ourselves in this way, we are telling ourselves that we are not good enough. How in the hell are you supposed to go on a date with someone you barely know—and truly connect with them—if you are thinking that you do not measure up? What if there was another way to relate to your body? If we take a step back and look at the big picture, we can see that our bodies are really only vessels to help us get from one place to another. The body serves as a vehicle, a physical entity that allows us to interact with our environment. It is an amazing and complex structure. We live in it. We should respect it and care for it. When we are critical of our bodies, we minimize its purpose and reduce it to simply being an object.

"The body serves as vehicle or a physical entity that allows us to interact with our environment."

Learning to appreciate all that your body is—and all that it can do—by practicing mindfulness gives you a different perspective. This new perspective can lead to a new regard for your body, which may help you begin to take care of your body in the way it deserves.

Mindful dating offers you the power to break free of the negative thoughts, overwhelming feelings, and destructive behaviors that cause you so much pain; it provides an alternative to the stressful, disappointing, lonely dating traps so many people fall into. You gain the ability to provide yourself with much-needed support, kindness, and understanding—while building a stronger sense of self. As you become more familiar with yourself and learn to handle yourself with care, you start to feel happier, more confident, and in control.

By attending to yourself in this way and cultivating more mindfulness, you create the opportunity to respond to your own needs, authentically connect with your date and suffer less. With these obstacles removed, the possibility for an enjoyable experience becomes more likely—and disappointing dates are seen for what they are instead of becoming a larger representation of your worst fears. But the most important benefit of mindful dating is the ability to let your genuine self emerge. This is your most attractive self. This is how real relationships with actual staying power are formed.

2 THE GREAT ESCAPE FROM THE DATING TRAP (THE ART OF MINDFUL DATING)

If you feel like you are in a dating rut, you are not alone. I have heard many people complain about feeling as if they are on a hamster wheel—they are getting nowhere fast, and they're frustrated, tired, hopeless, and downright cranky about it. Add the fact that you are probably unaware of why things are the way they are, and we've got a recipe for disaster. I like to call this the dating trap. The dating trap is the hazardous act of engaging in similar behavioral patterns around dating or unhealthy relationships due to lack of awareness, unresolved issues, automatic thoughts, and core beliefs. Now, I don't believe for one hot second that you are doing this on purpose. You are unconsciously repeating a cycle that must end. But how do we break loose of this trap? Well, as with any art form, you must learn the steps, develop the skills ... and practice, practice, practice.

About a month ago, I became overwhelmed with the desire to do something I had never done before. For over fifteen years, I have been waiting for my husband to be ready to take dance lessons with me. Every year I've waited for him to surprise me with tango, swing, waltz, or cha cha classes. As I sat stewing in my own feelings of resentment, I had an epiphany: *I can take dance lessons on my own. Just because he is not ready doesn't mean I have to wait for him.* And so, I did it! I got into my cute dance outfit, walked into a beginner salsa class that had been going for two months already, and joined in. At first it was humiliating. But I did my best, caught on some, made some new friends, and had a new goal in life. I love it, and I know it can only get better with practice. The same is true with learning the art of mindful dating. You can learn to enjoy the process and escape the dating trap.

There are many different traps we can fall into while dating. Picture a beautiful flower garden on top of a minefield. You may want to run through that garden barefoot and sniff each beautiful blossom ... but if you do not have a map of where those mines are planted, you are bound to get blown out of the garden. As you learn to navigate the dating world, it is important for you to be aware of what these traps might be, where they may lie, and how to avoid stepping on them. These traps are called Dating Devices. A device is a weapon that explodes. In dating, these devices can stand alone, or they may be present with other devices. Knowing your devices helps you to be less clumsy in your dating experiences and approach it from a more creative, authentic, and graceful place.

The dating trap is the hazardous act of engaging in similar behavioral patterns around dating or unhealthy relationships due to lack of awareness, unresolved issues, automatic thoughts, and core beliefs.

The steps to this art form are clear. You have already taken the first step. By reading this book, you have accepted that there is a problem that needs to be addressed. You are on your way to mindful dating. You must next learn what traps you are prone to fall into. We do not all have the same devices because we are not a homogenous people. We come from different backgrounds, have had different experiences, want different things and have different personalities. However, over the years I have come to recognize and categorize a few common pitfalls. Knowing your traps allows you to avoid them. Next, you must become acquainted with the principals of mindful dating. These include learning to date in the moment, using your breath, identifying your thought errors or dating distortions, and discovering how to freely feel. Then you must do some prep work for mindful dating by nurturing yourself and developing a stronger relationship with yourself. I find the self-care you will engage in during this step to be not only rewarding, but necessary to being emotionally fit for dating. Finally, we will put the pieces together and practice the skills of mindful dating.

In this chapter we will look at the different types of dating devices you might be walking right into. You may have one or you may have a bunch of them. By taking this next step, you begin to develop awareness around what has been holding you back. Let's take a look at the most common ones.

DATING DEVICES

The following section contains ten deadly relationship-killing dating devices that you should be aware of:

- Confusing sex for compatibility
- Personal branding
- Forgetting to look inside the box
- Living in La-la Land
- Being overly partner-centered
- I need a hero
- Lovin' love
- Stocking up
- Miss Independent
- Take me as I am

I developed these dating devices after years of using David Steele's book *Conscious Dating* with my clients. As I began working more with relationship issues and the problems my clients were facing while dating, Steele's fourteen "Dating Traps" served as a helpful tool, but over the years, I modified what I learned from him and tailored it toward the people I was encountering in my practice and personal life.

Now, don't worry if you see yourself in a few of these. Awareness is the key to making positive change in your life. Try being open the possibility that you are falling into some of these traps so we can get to work on that love life of yours! First up ...

Confusing Sex for Compatibility

Britney Spears was openly smitten with back-up dancer Kevin Federline in the mid-2000s. Their high-profile relationship exploded onto the scene, and neither one of them was ashamed about their sexual attraction to each other. It seemed obvious that these two were having sex and really enjoying it. They couldn't keep their hands off each other. They had a very strong sexual connection that led to an impulsive and short-lived marriage, two children, and a highly publicized custody battle. Now, I don't know Britney personally, but as an outside observer it seemed to me like our favorite pop princess made the age-old mistake of confusing great sex with compatibility—and she paid the price. Luckily, it seems Britney has rebounded, matured and found herself in more positive relationships since. So how can you avoid singing "Oops, I did it again" when it comes to this dating device?

You may not have said it out loud to anyone—or even admitted it to yourself yet. But if you find you have a history of becoming attached to sexual relationships that do not lead to long-term commitments, then you may be mistaking sex for compatibility. If the sex is good then the relationship will be good, right? Not necessarily. Sex can be its own thing entirely. Sex does not have to coexist with love for it to be physically satisfying. Yet, I have found many people who confuse the two things and continue to fail at relationships. The false belief that sex equals compatibility can lead to your ignoring red flags that indicate the relationship is doomed to fail. One way we can do this is by placing so much importance on the mere fact that we are having sex that we excuse behaviors that show a lack of commitment, compatibility, or respect. Some of us even take this a step further and convince ourselves that if we are having sex with someone we are in a committed relationship with them. We become invested in this belief without even having a conversation with our partner.

Another reason people get caught up in sex is purely biological. When you are sexually attracted to someone, all kinds of hormones, neurotransmitters, and chemicals start to surge in your body. Studies show it only takes from about a minute and a half to four minutes for you to decide whether or not you are attracted to someone. During this phase, testosterone and estrogen are driving your lust and creating more sexual desire. Norepinephrine is also produced and acts as a natural mood enhancer. Studies of MRI scans even show that the brain lights up when you are experiencing lust in the same way it does when you are on cocaine. Lust is like a drug in a lot of ways. When you start to explore your lust and enter the attraction phase, adrenalin, dopamine, and serotonin are bouncing around inside of you. Adrenaline is what makes you feel a little sweaty and nervous. Dopamine floods you with intense feelings of pleasure. Serotonin keeps your new lover on your mind, often in an idealized way, making you feel a little obsessed. And when you finally get to knockin' boots, your body releases the bonding hormone oxytocin, making you feel closer to your partner. It is easy to see how you can get out of touch with reality under the circumstances. Being solely focused on how you feel is clearly not the best way to assess compatibility.

Here in the US, we see sex all around us in television commercials about Viagra, on billboards for Victoria's Secret ads, or on the radio with songs that tell us he wants to "lick, lick, lick, lick, lick us like a lollipop." However, we receive all of these messages in a society that is still largely conservative when it comes to sex. Talking about sex and all of its implications—positive and negative—is still taboo. So we see sex and we think about sex … but we do not talk about it. This puts everyone in the awkward position of trying to figure things out on their own. As a result, there can be many misunderstandings about sex and love. One misunderstanding is that lust and love are the same thing. As we have discussed, lust is basically like a drug that squashes common sense and makes you idealize your partner and project your own feelings of attachment on to them. Lust is a fantasy state. Lust happens quickly. Love takes the time to get to know someone better. But love is not necessarily indicative of compatibility either. Sex does not equal love, and love does not equal happily ever after. Love can be influenced by attraction, feeling attached, or infatuation. But these feelings can wear off in time. That is why it is important to base compatibility on more than just sex. Compatibility is based on your values, goals, and relationship requirements—in addition to sexual chemistry and love. Good sex can be the start of a good relationship, but it is certainly not a guarantee of a successful relationship. If you are mindful of how sex can affect the way you think and feel—while keeping your relationship goals, values, and requirements in mind—you can be well on your way to developing a harmonious and successful relationship.

Personal Branding

When you are meeting or getting to know someone, it is natural to want to be liked and to make a good impression. We do this by putting on make-up, finding the perfect outfit, and wearing perfume. We also do this by managing our presentation of ourselves. There is no harm in putting forth some effort, right? In general, it doesn't hurt to try to be the best version of ourselves. But when it comes to dating, this can be a slippery slope—especially if you are desperate for things to work out. Being needy can cause us to hide who we are and cover up what we may consider to be our most undesirable qualities: our fears, flaws, insecurities, feelings, past mistakes—and even things we enjoy that we worry will not be received well by others. Dating is about getting to know each other, but if you try to present your personal "brand," by presenting a false version of yourself, you make it impossible for your date to get to know the real you and set yourself up for failure. Your presentation need not be strategic when you are truly aiming for an authentic relationship.

I see personal branding a lot among my clients. It often occurs with the ones who have become desperate to find love. Attitude counts for a lot when it comes to dating. If you are thinking that this has to work out, then you are likely to want to position yourself in the most flattering light, omitting who you truly are and being overly agreeable with the person you are with. That neediness can be detected easier than Christina Aguilera's weave tracks in 2002. So instead of presenting ourselves in a flattering way, by trying too hard, we are showing that we are uncomfortable with who we are and desperate to be liked. Does that sound like someone you want to date? Didn't think so.

Leading with our personal branding has another important impact on a potential relationship. It shifts the power dynamic between the two of you. Essentially, when you force a connection by being too adaptive—and by concealing who you are—you give all the power to the other person. What they want is important. What they like is important. Who they are is important. When Prince Akeem of Zamunda was presented with his bride in the comedy classic *Coming to America*, he was less than enthusiastic about what stood before him. Wanting to get to know this stunning woman, he asked a series of questions about her and what she likes to do. Her response to every question was a variation of "whatever you like." "Whatever kind of music you like." "Whatever food you like." And so on. This is an extreme example of what I mean, but you get the point. Being focused only on what the other person wants or likes leaves no room for what you want or like, and you relinquish your power in the relationship. In the long run, this is not a likable quality. It sets you up to be a doormat—and eventually resentful.

Additionally, when we don't represent ourselves authentically, we lose the ability to be who we truly are. By concealing our flaws, we trap ourselves into playing a role that we cannot sustain, and we lose sight of the whole point of dating: getting to know each other. Ultimately, the false presentation we are so focused on actually makes us less attractive and appealing. What is attractive about someone who is ashamed of who they really are and is willing to give up the power in the relationship just to be liked?

Though it may seem like a paradox, the truth is that self-acceptance and authenticity are what makes someone appealing. Being at peace with who you are—including your flaws, mistakes, fears, and so on—makes you personable and engaging. And if you are *not* at peace with these qualities, just accepting that fact—and owning it—is more appealing than hiding your true self. This means you must learn to be comfortable with who you are, including your flaws. Be yourself.

Forgetting to Look Inside the Box

When I was a kid, I remember my mother's boyfriend receiving a huge, beautifully wrapped birthday present. There was a giant bow on it, and we could not imagine what was inside. He tore off the wrapping paper, cut through the tape on the box, and opened it up … only to find a slightly smaller box inside. The suspense was killing me! *What is in there?* I thought to myself. He opened that box … and guess what was inside? Another slightly smaller box. I watched him repeat the process three or four more times.

When he got to the final box, he pulled out a bottle of Pepto Bismol. It was an unoriginal but well-crafted joke that taught me a good lesson. Never judge a gift by the packaging. Underneath all that shiny paper and bows could be diarrhea medication. The same is true for dating.

The laws of attraction are simple. We attract what we are focused on. We usually talk about the laws of attraction in reference to bringing about life experiences or events through our positive or negative thinking. If we think positively, then positive things will manifest in our lives. If we think negatively, those thoughts become a self-fulfilling prophecy. These laws apply to dating as well. Being focused on the surface presentation of a date will attract people who fit some of the criteria, but do not fulfill our needs. I often hear people talk to me about the kind of person they want to be with in terms of their outward appearance, their job, how much money they have, and their material possessions. I am not here to tell you that you should not have standards. However, when these external factors are the things you are focused on, you can overlook many more important qualities that can have a serious impact on the fate of your relationship. It is what is inside the box that really matters. Is this person kind, generous, a good listener, or funny? Do we have things in common? Do I feel safe around them? Are they married? (Who knows? You were so smitten by Joe Manganiello sitting across from you that you forgot to ask!)

Ciara is one of my clients, an attractive African American woman in her mid-thirties, with a natural hairstyle and sassy personality. She is focused on upward mobility in her current company, but she also feels she is ready for a relationship. She has been guarded in recent years due to fear of rejection. But something else has also held her back from forming connections. She has a belief that money is power. She grew up in an environment where this was reinforced by financial instability and dependence on others. She doesn't need a partner to be independently wealthy, but she has a hard time taking someone seriously if they do not have their finances tight. When we explored how this has impacted her dating life, she cited a recent interaction with an old flame who had expressed interest in her again. They had a very strong connection—spiritually and emotionally. She felt great when she was with him, and she found him attractive. However, he was a musician and financially unstable. He was not struggling, but he did not have a clear financial plan drawn up. Because of this, she blew him off, disregarding all the positive attributes he had that could have formed a strong foundation for a healthy relationship. This automatic response to him left her feeling regretful—and as if she had missed an opportunity. In this case, the box was not presentable even though the contents were just what she was looking for. Ciara placed more value on one specific superficial quality of her date than on the many other attributes that were of true value to her. With mindfulness, she might have responded to this automatic reaction and seen what she was really looking for inside the box.

For some of us there is another reason why we do not look inside the box. When we are dazzled by the perfectly wrapped package, it can be easy to get caught up in the way we are being evaluated. Cue your inner monologue: *Is he interested? How can I make sure he is interested? I hope he likes me.* So you are engaging and talkative, responding to every inquiry and doing your best to make sure that he likes you ... and you forget one important thing: to get to know him as well. This can make your date feel somewhat alienated, neglected, and uninteresting. In addition, it can lead to an unsteady rhythm in the date and can keep you two out of sync. This shift in the natural rhythm may prevent a true connection from being formed. You were so focused on making it work that you worked yourself right out of second date! Or even worse, you worked yourself into a second date with someone who is not a good match!

The only way to make a true long-lasting connection with someone is to become familiar with them—inside and out. A mindful approach incorporates paying attention to your thoughts and feelings in addition to your senses. This is necessary because compatibility is not about what someone looks like or what he has. It is about who he really is and how you feel with him. Being attracted to your date is important, and chemistry should not be overlooked ... but it takes much more than that to create a sustainable and successful romance.

Living in La-La Land

I cannot tell you how many times I have heard people tell me that love should not be so hard. You should not have to put so much effort into a finding a relationship. If it is meant to be, love will come to you. That is the biggest load of crap I have ever heard! If Tula would have stayed a mousy hostess at the Dancing Zorba's in *My Big Fat Greek Wedding*, she would have never found love, and we would not have the greatest romantic comedy in history. A successful relationship may just show up for some people, but believing that it will just appear out of thin air for you is like waiting to win the lottery. If you subscribe to this belief, you are living in la-la land.

When it comes to finding love, you cannot take a hands-off approach. If you want to be in a successful relationship, you have to be on the hunt. Believing that love will just happen places you in a passive role when you are about to make some very personal decisions. Shouldn't you have more of a say in whom you date, besides simply responding "yes" or "no" to whatever dude shows interest in you? This takes you completely out of the selection process and will most likely lead to disappointing date after disappointing date with people you are incompatible with. Or it could even lead to no dates at all because you are not actively looking. Whatever it leads to, it is not going to lead to the unrealistic happily-ever-after you are dreaming of.

Mindfulness is about observing, taking in all of the information around you and then actively making a choice. A successful partnership requires you to be a part of the process. You must be aware of what you are looking for in a partner and learn to recruit potential partners. You must be aware of what you can bring to a relationship and own who you are. You must take responsibility for the choices you are making—and for the results—instead of blaming others. You must learn how to separate the mighty good men from the scrubs. You must stop waiting to be approached. Step away from the gym wall at your junior high school dance, and ask the guy with the moves you like to dance with you.

Being Overly Partner-Centered

We all have that friend or family member who is always in a relationship but never quite happy in it. In fact, they are miserable, often preoccupied with relationship worries and complaining about their issues—and you wonder to yourself, *Why don't they just leave?* Or, they might never complain ... but you can sense their anxiety around the relationship, and it is easy to see that they are not fulfilled. If you do not know him or her, then it is possible that *you* are that person I am talking about. In any case, there are many reasons why people stay in relationships that are not good for them such as financial constraints, family pressure, shared children, and more. I will focus on one fairly common reason why I have seen people stay boo'ed up under these circumstances. They are needy and want a relationship so badly—because they feel inadequate and broken without one. And they do so at any cost—while sacrificing their needs and desires.

Being selfless in a relationship—and putting your partner's needs ahead of your own—is what relationships are all about, right? Absolutely not! Yes, we may do this in relationships, but if you are the person who is always providing support to your partner but not receiving support back ... there is a problem. No relationship should be lopsided in this way. If this behavior becomes a pattern, you will find you are sacrificing more than your time and energy for your partner's happiness. This type of codependency requires payment in your mental, emotional, and physical health. Think about it ... if you are pushing your needs to the side to take care of your partner, then when will you have time for yourself? Partner-pleasing like this can lead to depression, anxiety, stress, and a bunch of other mental health issues. If you let your partner cross your boundaries sexually, if you are engaged in an abusive relationship, or if you simply cannot prioritize your basic self-care needs (think exercise, eating, sleep, doctors' appointments, spending time with friends, etc.), then your physical health is in danger. If you are constantly giving and not receiving, this may affect your emotional health and lead to you feeling unworthy, insecure, sad, anxious, frustrated, angry, and more. Forfeiting these parts of yourself not only has an impact on you, but it can also be harmful to your partner. If your sacrifices somehow enable dysfunctional behaviors, such as drinking or dependency, you are not doing your partner any favors.

People who are extra-focused on their relationship often convince themselves that they are doing so because they are loving, supportive, and needed. But there is usually a deeper explanation for their behavior—being partner-centered in a relationship is often a result of being insecure with who you are. By giving so much of yourself and blindly complying with your partner's wishes, you establish a relationship in which you are needed by your partner—and this validates your self-worth. This creates a vicious cycle of being needy for your partner's attention and giving too much of yourself to keep your partner on the hook. You are in the position of needing to be needed, which makes you just as dependent on your partner as your partner is on you. In addition, a partner who is so dependent on you will be unable to give you the things you need. Not having your needs met will likely result in feeling insecure, which leads you back to needing your partner's approval to feel validated. As you can see, the partner-centered cycle is vicious!

The compulsive need to be with a specific person to feel complete and happy at any cost is another symptom of being partner-centered. Think of Edward and Bella in the *Twilight* saga. As captivated by this love affair as we were, there were some serious codependency issues driving the plot. Edward could not stop thinking about Bella. From the time he first rescued her and got a whiff of her intoxicating scent, she was the only thing on his mind. Obsessed much? He needed to be around her to the extent that he would set up camp in her bedroom to watch her sleep. He referred to Bella as his own personal brand of heroin. Bella became so engrossed in the relationship that she thought nothing of giving up her friends, dismissing her father's concerns, and changing her entire life and identity so they could be together. This kind of behavior was viewed as passionate by the characters and audience alike, but the truth is: this relationship was clearly unhealthy for both Edward and Bella! No one should give themselves up to be in a relationship. When you finally start to see unhealthy behaviors in your partner—or when things turn sour or become abusive in some way and you are left with nothing of your own—this behavior will only make it that much more difficult to leave the relationship, and you will end up feeling trapped and resentful.

Someone who is partner-centered often experiences difficulty identifying and expressing their own needs, desires, and boundaries. In fact, having poor boundaries—or none at all—is a major part of the problem. Boundaries help you to separate yourself from someone else. Without boundaries it becomes more likely that you will take on your partner's problems as your own. Poor boundaries make it hard for you to detach your feelings from your partner's feelings. What is yours becomes your partner's too— even if it means you have given him your Metro card and your last dollar and your ass now has to walk to work.

For a relationship to be healthy and successful, you cannot lose yourself or give yourself to your partner. It is necessary for any partnership, especially a romantic one, to be based on both people's needs, wants, and requirements. If you struggle with identifying what these are, then this is an essential place to start. Learn how to express yourself and assert your boundaries. Make sure your character and sense of self is not determined by what your partner thinks, but by what you think. Discover how to feel complete by yourself. Make sure your partner wants the same things you do. Assess whether your needs are being met in the relationship. Become more discerning about whom you date! And keep in mind that it takes two people to be in a partner-centered relationship. Take time to think about whether you are the one in the relationship controlling, manipulating, crossing boundaries, or depending on your partner to take care of needs you should be taking responsibility for.

I Need a Hero

Hailey, a twenty-four-year-old Colombian American woman born and raised in New York City, came to therapy due to depression and relationship issues with her current boyfriend. Before they started dating, Hailey did not have many friends, spent a lot of time alone, often felt lonely, had very low self-esteem and believed her lack of money held her back from changing any of this. So she decided that a relationship would fix these issues. It took a few months, but a relationship is what she got. They have been together for five years now, and when things started, they were great. Hailey and her new steady did everything together. Hailey finally had plans on the weekends. Her boyfriend paid for everything. They spent all their time together, and she did not feel lonely anymore. However, over time she started to realize that they were not a good match in many ways. She began to feel even more isolated from people because her boyfriend demanded so much of her time. She only did the things her boyfriend would fund—which made her feel resentful. She gained a lot of weight because her boyfriend, who paid for everything, did not eat healthily and had no intention of changing his diet. She became depressed and angry over time, and when she expressed herself in the relationship they would fight—and things would escalate and become verbally abusive. More recently, things escalated to the point where they became physically volatile as well.

Hailey felt trapped in the relationship with no means to get out. In our last session, she came up with an escape plan that she claimed had lifted her depression in the past week. She decided she would sleep with her next-door neighbor, who is a nice guy, and get pregnant ... and he would take care of her and the baby, allowing her to finally leave her current relationship.

Hailey is an extreme example of the I Need a Hero dating device. She believes that a relationship can solve all her problems. She looks to others to rescue her from social, emotional, and financial peril. However, when you make someone else responsible for your happiness, you are subject to their rule. What they say goes. At first, this might seem desirable ... but in time you will inevitably begin to feel bitter toward your partner who is only participating in the dynamic you helped to create. You will start to feel trapped by the relationship and may blame your partner for all of your problems. And the problems you initially had that seemed to disappear will surface again and double—or even triple. In Hailey's case, she now had a contentious and abusive relationship to navigate, trouble seeing any way out, safety issues to think about, health issues, increased emotional instability, and dependency on her partner—in addition to her original problem of being socially isolated, feeling lonely, and having few financial resources.

The other major problem with this device is that other people cannot know what you need to be happy. They have their own needs and desires to attend to. In most cases, when you lead with this line of thinking, you are likely to come off as needy and desperate. As a result, you will either repel good candidates to date—or attract those who can give you that instant gratification but who are less suitable partners in the long run. Your happiness is your responsibility. Only you can figure out what will make you feel satisfied and fulfilled. Assuming that a relationship or an individual will provide you with happiness is quick way to end up defeated. Even in a seemingly healthy partnership, this expectation will cause problems and drive a wedge between the two of you. It just does not work!

The solution to this dating device is pretty simple. You should not seek a relationship until you feel complete on your own. Make it your mission to figure out how to provide yourself with satisfaction, happiness, and fulfillment. Be open to new experiences and mindful of what brings you a sense of joy. Approach this task with curiosity, and enjoy the process instead of being focused on the end goal. Your independence is an essential part of your feeling whole—in or out of a relationship. You will know your value when it is time to start dating and will be less likely to end up with someone who is not a good fit.

Lovin' Love

I love love as much as anybody else. Or so I thought. As I became more experienced as a therapist, and as I began observing the people in my life, I noticed there was definitely a difference between the way I loved love and the way some other folks were doing it. Some were so in love with love—and placed so much value on that feeling of infatuation—that they forgot to dig a little deeper. Therefore they found themselves in committed relationships very quickly. Things were blissful ... until they were not. Inevitably problems would arise, and these folks would oftentimes be shocked by this. If any of this sounds familiar to you, then you might be a victim of the Lovin' Love dating device.

When you meet that certain someone who sends your heart fluttering, it is hard not to jump ahead of yourself and imagine how wonderful life would be together. Sometimes there is an immediate chemistry that ignites when you meet someone new. It seems like you just get each other. Then you learn that you guys both love the NY Giants, artisanal pizza, cross-fit, and dystopian fiction novels—and you are convinced that this is the one. So you jump right in, headfirst. The problem is you did not spend enough time getting to know him. Yes, you guys have a lot in common, and there is definitely chemistry ... but it takes a while for you to really get to know someone. Six months into the relationship—when you find out that there are some serious differences in the way you envision your family planning, and that he expects you to put your career on hold to have his five children—you are heartbroken and confused about how you could have been so wrong about him. The truth is, you did not really know him. To assume that a long-term relationship will work based on surface things you have in common and on a feeling, as strong as it may be, is foolish.

Another common mistake I see from those who are just Lovin' Love is valuing someone's potential over what is there in front of you. Cheryl and Gary dated on-and-off for over three years. There was true affection between the two of them, and they enjoyed spending time together. When things were good, they were amazing, but Gary had trouble staying committed in the relationship and often cheated. They would briefly separate, but not for long. Cheryl always took him back because she saw what a good man he was when things were going well. She also knew how intelligent he was; they had met in college, and they had many intellectually stimulating conversations. However, Gary dropped out of college to work more hours in his stock job at Trader Joe's. He was less than a year away from a degree in science and technology when he dropped out, and Cheryl just knew he would find his way back to school. Cheryl was right that Gary was intelligent; he did care for her and he was a good man when things were going well. She saw all of his potential and hoped that he would change if he loved her. She worked overtime to get that loving feeling back. However, Cheryl did not take the time to evaluate his motivation, his desire to commit fully to the relationship, and his life goals. She also waited too long into the relationship to discuss what her expectations were. By the time they had this discussion, they were two years into dating, and Cheryl focused on making things work even though they were clearly incompatible. When Gary finally admitted in therapy that he was unsure if he could be faithful, and that he was not interested in returning to school, Cheryl was heartbroken. It took some time for Cheryl to understand that it takes more than love and potential for a relationship to work. Had Cheryl been upfront about her expectations and desires in the beginning of the relationship, she might have avoided spending so much time with a partner who was not on the same page as she was.

A relationship is not something to jump right into, even if the love is there. It takes time to get to know someone and for them to get to know you. Expectations should be discussed. Values should be shared. Relationship goals should be addressed. Your requirements need to be clear to you and your partner before you take that next step. You wouldn't buy a new car without figuring out what you want, negotiating the price, and taking it for a test drive. Obviously, even more thought and time need to go into entering a long-term relationship.

Stocking Up

I am from Los Angeles, California, where we do not have very many natural disasters to worry about. Well, except for a little thing called earthquakes. But the thing about earthquakes is that while they are terrifying, you do not get any warning about when they will strike. So you are taught to always have an earthquake kit full of drinkable water, a battery-operated radio, batteries, a flashlight, etc. When I moved to New York City and was faced with my first snowstorm, I soon learned that when you find out about an impending natural disaster you are supposed to go into frenzied high-alert mode. Whether it is a hurricane or a snowstorm, you first panic and then drag your ass down to the local market and stock up on everything you will need should the worst happen. You'd better get there quick because there are 11 million other panicked New Yorkers scrambling to be prepared as well, and you will have no one to blame but yourself when you go to the bread aisle and see that the only kind left on the shelves is rye olive loaf. When the snow melts or the hurricane passes, you are left with a cabinet full of Spaghetti Os and ten loaves of rye bread—and no desire to eat any of it.

A similar pattern exists among some single folks. I have noticed that there are some people that believe there is not enough stock out there, and their anxiety about becoming an "old maid" leads them to stocking up on a partner. As I have heard it put before, you are so worried that there are not enough fish in the sea that you settle for any clown fish that comes your way.

This distorted view of dating is more common than you may think, but most of us do not know we are thinking this way. That is because it is deeply hidden in our psyche, making us unaware of this driving thought. The underlying belief is that there are not enough folks to go around, and if you do not hurry up and snag a partner, you will be left alone. But approaching dating in this way sets you up for disaster. First of all, what do you think happens when you are convinced that you better get boo'd up before all the potential partners are taken? Like I stated before, you end up settling for what is easiest for you to get. Proximity or accessibility is valued over quality. Yes, you have an immediate cuddle bunny … but when you settle you do not get the partner you want—you get the partner that was there. In most cases this person does not measure up to the person you envisioned yourself with. When you accept a relationship with just anyone, even though someone else would be better, you set yourself for certain failure.

Another possible consequence of thinking about relationships in this way is that you never really give the person you are with a fair chance. That is because you have settled for something you are not truly satisfied with. That person's flaws become glaringly apparent and you are overly aware of how they do not measure up. As a result, you are always looking for someone a little better. When you find that person, you are on to the next one, but still not getting the partner you want because they are the next lowest hanging fruit … all worm-ridden and bruised, but you don't care because "at least you got a man."

I work with and am around a lot of black women, and I see this phenomenon occurring quite frequently with us. I grew up being told by several people throughout my life that there was only one "good" black man for every ten black women. I read an article recently that stated this statistic had grown to three "good" black men for every hundred women! If that is not enough to send you into a stockpiling panic, I don't know what is.

Samantha, an educated, Ethiopian-American long-term client of mine in her thirties, had dated often with little to no success. She wanted to be with a black man, but because her standards were so low, she found herself in relationships with men who were not deserving of her. She has been cheated on, stolen from, emotionally abused, and exploited. This is certainly not because there are no good black men. I know many successful, attractive, eligible black men who would have made great partners for Samantha. The real explanation for this is that Samantha, like many women of any ethnicity, believed that she had an insufficient supply of suitable partners and was then not sufficiently discerning about whom she dated.

The only way to get what you want in a relationship is to know what you want and to go after it. I am not saying that it will be easy, but with some tenacity and a belief that you can get what you want, you are much more likely to be successful than if you subscribe to this tired belief that you have to "get what you can get." I've told my eight-year-old daughter many times that "You get what you get and you don't get upset." This does not, however, apply to dating. If what you are getting is upsetting, it is time to think about what you want, exercise your power to choose, and be ready when Mr. or Ms. Right comes your way so you can snag that catch!

Miss Independent

You want a partner, but you certainly do not need one. No one actually needs to have a partner, right? You are independent. If something needs to be fixed, you are on it. If you see a new pair of stilettos you love, you buy them for yourself. And if something needs heavy lifting and is too much for you to handle, you know the service to call to get the job done. You can take care of yourself. But is it possible that you have become so independent that you do not have room in your life for the partner you truly desire? Let's examine this further.

A lot of dating advice tells you that you should know what you want in a relationship, and you do. As Miss Independent, you know exactly what you want, and you won't subject yourself to riffraff. In fact, your screening process has become so developed that you are able to spot a loser a mile away. Phew, you dodged a bullet there! Well maybe ... but you are also missing out on a whole lot by being so judgmental, protective, and cautious. Your independence has become a fortress, keeping out more than just the unsuitable suitor. In fact, if your brand of independence is so laser-focused on what you do not want and how people do not measure up, you may be overlooking people who may make good partners—or even who could be a good friend. It is easy to see how this way of approaching dating can cause you to feel isolated and lonely.

To make things even more complicated, your rigid requirements can make it impossible for any one person to meet them all. It is certainly important not to settle, but you have taken this to an extreme, and because nobody can meet your standards, you may start to see the dating pool as extremely limited. If no one can fulfill your requirements, you may believe this is indicative of there not being enough of a supply of "good" guys out there. This way of thinking leaves you vulnerable to the "stocking up" device when the loneliness becomes more than you can bear. Ironically, the very thing you have been protecting yourself from, settling, is exactly what you end up doing.

For some of us, this independence can take a different shape. You may have created a great life for yourself! It is full of good friends, interesting hobbies and fun activities. And when I say full, I mean F-U-L-L. There is no room for dating because your days are jam-packed with stuff to do. It is likely that if this is your lifestyle, you probably think that love will come to you. If you are doing the things you love, then you will stumble upon the guy of your dreams doing those same things, right? Picture it: you are in yoga, doing downward-facing dog when you notice a handsome stranger behind you. He is slower at his *vinyasa*, so you lock eyes with him while he is in cobra … and the rest is history! Sounds great, huh? Yeah, but it is also a fantasy. Wake up! Your independence has led you to be complacent about actively finding love—and that most likely will not end up in your happily-ever-after.

In addition to becoming complacent about looking for love, your independence may have another effect on your potential to find a partner. When you are so busy and independent, others may sense there is no room in your life for a partner. Demi Lovato asks, "What's wrong with being confident?" The answer, of course, is nothing. Confidence is a beautiful thing! However, you may think you are projecting confidence and self-sufficiency, but the vibe being transmitted may be closer to "I don't need a man." That subtle difference can make a big impact. The truth is we all need each other. Whether it is good friends or a partner, we humans are social beings who crave connection, affection, and support. If you are giving off the vibe that you do not need anyone, you are fooling everybody—including yourself.

The point here is that it is okay to want a relationship. It is normal and natural to want to have an intimate connection. It is great that you can take care of yourself, but for any partnership to work, there has to be give and take. At some point you will need to allow your partner to take care of you, and vice versa. Depending on your partner is not the same as depending on someone to provide you happiness and fulfillment or being codependent. Reciprocity in a relationship is healthy and desirable. Keep your independent spirit and pair it with openness. Stop making dating a second-rate priority when you know a relationship is important to you. Let go of your rigid requirements while still being mindful of the things that are important to you, and make room in your life for a special someone who can enhance it.

Take Me as I Am

When it comes to dating, there seems to be the belief among some of us that we deserve to get the person we want—no matter who that person is.

You have extraordinary taste and only want the best for yourself, and that includes the most desirable partner. The problem is you do not possess the same attributes—or even parallel attributes in some other but equally important area. You do not think you should have to change to get the partner you want. You believe you are owed the best without having to put in any work or make any self-improvements. Well, wake up! This is not how real life works. And I will tell you why.

Now, I have heard people who fall victim to the Take Me as I Am device use the saying "Opposites attract." Yes, that is true sometimes ... but opposites implies equal—not just different. In Paula Abdul's hit song, MC Skat Cat spits some wisdom that cannot be denied. He says, "I'm like a minus, she's like a plus. One coming up, one coming down, but we seem to land on common ground." In this example, Skat Cat is showing us that they may have differences but they end up in the same place because they are equally opposing forces that balance each other out. He also says, "When things go wrong we make corrections, to keep things moving in the right direction." This is in absolute conflict with the idea that you should not have to change to get the partner you want. For you, when things go wrong you stay the same because you don't think you should have to change. But most of you won't even get this far because you won't make the changes necessary to get a potential relationship off the ground or make yourself an attractive candidate.

When you get rejected or lack dating success, it inevitably leads to anger and resentment toward your dating pool—men or women, depending on your preference. And why wouldn't it? Nobody likes to be rejected over and over again. Eventually, you begin lashing out at your dating pool—or even worse, you give up and deem the whole thing hopeless. The perfect person you are dreaming of eludes you, so you protect yourself by throwing in the towel, forever sealing your fate. You sabotage yourself throughout the entire dating process, from beginning to end, by refusing to make some adjustments that can improve your chances.

Other possible outcomes of this belief have to do with the way you interact with potential partners. Being repeatedly rejected makes you view your entire dating pool as evil, untrustworthy, cunning dogs who only objectify women. Instead of looking at how your presumptuous approach may be off-putting, you externalize the blame and characterize potential partners as upholding the dirty, dishonorable, or unfair structure of dating. Sooner or later, this makes interacting with them impossible. Instead of developing a personal connection, you look at each interaction as an opportunity to prove your virtue and beat the system! Dating becomes a game for you that can only be won if you are able to control the person you are interested in by making *them* interested. This usually goes one of two ways. One: You behave in a grandiose way, placing yourself above the person you are talking to, being argumentative and demanding. Two: You are manipulative and fake—lying about who you are and what your intentions are, to trick your admired one into being interested in you. As you can probably guess, neither one of these options results in romantic bliss. And more rejection, disappointment, and emotional turmoil only serve to deepen your belief that it is them and not you who are the problem.

When you believe you are entitled to love, happiness, and romantic partnership, you are doing yourself a major disservice. Ultimately, your assumptions end up biting you in the butt and lead you toward self-sabotage. The solution to this problem is to take responsibility for your role in the problem. Get a clue. If you are doing the same thing and getting the same results when dating, then it is time to accept that it is *not* them—it is you! If you want a 10, you have to be a 10. Work on self-improvement, and become the type of person who can attract the type of partner you have your eyes set on. Be realistic about who is in your dating pool. Learn to relate to potential partners as equals, without having to put yourself in a position of power. Accept that you may make mistakes—and that this is okay. Do this for real and not just so you can close the deal. You will be more satisfied with who you are—and believe that you are worthy of the relationship you want, instead of thinking you are entitled to one.

So which dating devices seem familiar to you? Most likely there is more than one that fits—and that can seem a little overwhelming. Do not be discouraged. This is true for most of us, but not everyone can identify why they have had such a hard time finding love. You are already ahead of the curve! Now that you know the patterns you tend to fall into when dating, you have learned the second step in this art form. You can identify what is and what is not working. You are more acquainted with your fears that are holding you back. You have become more self-aware, which will be very helpful moving forward. You are well on your way, so take time to acknowledge the progress you have made thus far. Be mindful of the effort you have put forth to learn more about your dating habits and make a positive change in your life.

3 YOU BE YOU: DATING OUTSIDE THE LINES

Spread love, it's the Brooklyn way.
—*Notorious BIG*

At first glance, it may look as though this book is written specifically for a particular audience: namely, women seeking partnership with a man. However, even if you do not fit the traditional prototype of the heteronormative conservative standard often endorsed by society, you can still benefit from the practices in this book. You may date outside the lines by choosing or being attracted to those who come from a different or similar gender identity or sexual orientation; different ethnic, religious, or cultural background; different type of family of origin; different marital status; differing age groups; different parenting history; different level of privilege and/or socioeconomic status; be differently abled; or hail from a different country of origin—just to scratch the surface. Considering all of the possible ways our unique identities and diverse backgrounds can make us different, it is my intention to provide universal mindful dating principles and exercises that highlight our similarities and are inclusive and practical for all.

To ignore that there are certain circumstances that present more of a challenge for some people than others would be irresponsible. Yes, at the heart, everything written in this and the other chapters applies wholeheartedly to anyone who reads it, but that does not mean that there are not particular challenges some people have to navigate in life. This is especially true with dating, where your private preferences and personal beliefs can become very public, opening you up to the possibility of being marginalized, gaslighted, discriminated against, or hurt by others. Though many may like to believe that we live in a society where all are created equal and everyone is given the rights and respect to be who they are, systematic racism and sexism, prejudices, and the historical shaming of lifestyles and backgrounds do exist and limit our ability to date freely. These pressures can affect our ability to find true happiness and acceptance of ourselves for fear of being judged, ostracized, abandoned, or even harmed by those we love. In addition, being different may open us up to people being attracted to you based on their own stereotypes, expectations, and prejudgments about who you are.

Heteronormative: referring to the belief that heterosexuality is the normal, preferred or given sexual orientation instead of it being one of many possibilities.

Dating outside of the lines can bring about a world of possibilities and may be necessary for you to find true inner peace, but it ain't always easy! I am not saying this book will address every type of dating situation or challenge out there but I do believe it will provide you with the necessary tools to navigate the sometimes threatening dating world in a healthy, open, and genuine way. Here are three key principles to keep in mind while dating outside of the lines: honesty, navigating needs, and managing outside opinions.

HONESTY

Honesty can seem tricky when it comes to dating. You do not want to divulge your deepest, darkest secrets to someone you are just meeting, but you also do not want to withhold important information that could affect the other person's ability to truly get to know you and make a well-informed decision about how they feel and what they think about you. *Eeeesh*, talk about being in a vulnerable position! But by finding the balance between over-sharing and being your genuine self, you yield the possibilities of finding a true connection.

LGBTQ: Lesbian, Gay, Bisexual, Transgender, and Queer/Questioning.

Honesty requires you to be open with those you are dating but also demands you be honest with yourself about who you are and where you at this stage in your life. If you identify as LGBTQ, for example, own what stage of coming out you are in. If you are fully out of the closet, no relationship is worth you forcing yourself back in for it. Similarly, if you are still not out and proud, do not push yourself to be somewhere you are not to satisfy your partner. To reduce the risk of this happening, consider dating someone who is in the same stage of coming out as you. This means being up front and owning where you are. Mindful dating is about being your authentic self, and same-sex couples must do their best to unapologetically do so in this case. If you are bisexual, be honest about that with whomever you are dating. If you are questioning or identify as queer, you should be genuine with your date about where you are in your life and how you identify. While there is no obligation to talk about your sexuality prior to going out on a date, it can make things pretty awkward if you do not talk about it and the relationship ends up becoming more serious. If you are not up front, some people might feel tricked or angry that you were not truthful. Your amazing journey is an important part of your story to share with a potential long-term partner early on, and that sharing can make for a real and deep connection.

Honesty can feel unsafe for some—especially for those who identify as transgender—because of the brutality and violence that they may face, sometimes daily. Assault, suicide, and murder are real risks that can make being honest right away very scary. It seems like we as a society in the United States have become much more accepting of those who identify as LGBTQ and some significant gains have been made, but there is still a lot of prejudice and hatred out there and we have a long way to go. This is one reason why having a community is so important. You can make sure your peeps have your back and know where you are and who is with you. This can be especially useful in the beginning of a relationship when you feel less safe and do not know the person very well. Nothing is risk-free, but you can do some harm reduction by dating people who know you are LGBTQ from the get-go. That means owning and disclosing your status online and via email, meeting people within your community, or being set up by friends who will be upfront about your identity as well. If someone has a negative reaction, you can avoid potentially uncomfortable or unsafe in-person encounters.

There are certainly additional obstacles when it comes to dating with a physical disability. Self-consciousness about what other people are thinking about you or how they see you can magnify any insecurities you may have. You may feel it's

> Queer: a positive label that captures the spirit of resisting cultural standards of what is "normal" gender and sexuality.

difficult to meet people who are willing to date someone with a disability. And once you do find an interested suitor, you may find yourself tempted to settle for a warm body. Whether you have a disability or not, when dating it is important for you to be aware of what your motivation is for finding a partner. Be honest with yourself about whether you are looking for a savior or a caregiver instead of a romantic partner. It can save you a lot of heartache. That is a shaky foundation for anyone to build a relationship on, and often leads to hurt and disappointment.

The same goes for anyone dating someone with a disability. If you have a tendency to be a caregiver and your attraction is partially based on following your own patterns, it is important for you to own this and think of the impact that this can have on your partner in the long-term. At first glance it may seem selfless and noble, but you can actually be putting yourself in a position to end up feeling resentful toward your partner. Motivation based on being a caregiver is often about your needs to sacrifice or feel good about yourself, or it can also be about receiving praise or sympathy. It is not completely about the person you are dating. You risk hurting your partner, who may think the basis of the relationship is mutual affection, attraction, and connection instead of your desire to be a "good person."

If you are considering dating after divorce, there is one important question you will want to ask yourself: Am I ready? You may be getting a lot of advice from friends and family to get back out there, find a rebound, or get your feet wet—but ultimately the only person who knows if you are ready to date is you. All of that pressure can be hard to put into perspective, and it can confuse you at times. If a short-term fling is something you are into, then go ahead and look for a quick hookup or someone to have on speed dial but not get too serious about. But if you are seeking a soulmate, then you will want to be mindful of how you are feeling about the possibility of getting coupled up again. It is important for you to have a good understanding of what went wrong—and what role you played in the demise of your marriage. You will be in much better shape to successfully date if you have a clear idea of what a healthy partnership looks like for you. You must be your authentic self when you are starting a new relationship, and if you are not ready to date, that is okay. Wait until you are, and you will get much better results.

Whether your relationship ended on a good or bad note, chances are you got pretty comfortable with your former life and routine. You may even be holding on to a lot of your former lifestyle, and this can make starting something new challenging and scary. Before you start dating, try stepping outside of your comfort zone and engaging in something new. This can be anything from joining a new organized sports team to getting a full hair and wardrobe makeover. It will help boost your confidence and get you used to interacting with new people. Dating again will be an adventure, and you need to be up for the new experiences you will encounter—and be able to handle them with openness and flexibility.

❁ ❁ ❁

Dating can also get very complicated when you are a single parent. But one way you can simplify things is by being honest about your family status. Always be upfront about having kids. This is not a second-, third-, or fourth-date conversation. Ideally, your date should know about your child before agreeing to go on a first date. Yes, this may thin out your dating pool, but it can save you from wasting your time with people who are not appropriate for you. Now, this does not mean that you have to spend your date talking about your kids and sharing pictures. But it should be very clear that you are a parent and that your kids are a priority in your life. This way they can decide whether or not they are willing to get involved with someone with your family circumstances. And you can weed out the jerks who have no interest in respecting your boundaries or developing a relationship with your kids (when you say the time is right).

Honesty about your religious or spiritual beliefs is also an important consideration. I have heard from many interfaith couples that they experience distress around their differing religious beliefs. On the surface, it seemed like there was no way they could make

"... get to know your own religious identity before you think about forcing it on your partner."

their relationship work when their families had such strong faith practices. They pushed each other to take on their individual rituals and customs. But over time they realized that they were pushing for something that they did not truly understand.

Many of us are raised in a specific religion and are taught from a young age how to be religious, but we don't fully grasp why we engage in such practices. We just do. This leaves us with little understanding of what we actually believe in and what is important to us. That is why it is important that you get to know your own religious identity before you think about forcing it on your partner. There may be aspects of your religious practices that you do not actually feel strongly about and others that you do. Being in tune with your own religious identity will allow you to share what is important to your partner and allow you to be curious and open to what they believe in.

NAVIGATING NEEDS

It is only natural to be swept away when you start dating someone you are really into. However, if you find that you are so focused on your partner that you have lost sight of your own needs, you are on a destructive path that will not lead to anything positive. In addition, you may have the responsibility of taking care of the needs of others, such as children, to consider. Navigating needs is an essential part of a well-rounded dating life that you must figure out ahead of time to ensure balance and healthy boundaries.

Community

Maintaining or creating a community for yourself may be an important piece of the puzzle for you and your needs. If you identify as LGBTQ but are not already involved in the LGBTQ community, I encourage you to get connected! There is a lot to gain from developing relationships with people who have had similar experiences, who have similar viewpoints, and who are accepting of each other's expression of their sexual orientation. You can benefit from the support you will receive and the sense of belonging that you may feel. You also open yourself up to making new connections that may create new possibilities for fulfillment, friendship, and romance.

If you have lost your spouse or are divorced (and depending on how long your marriage lasted), perhaps returning to the idea of seeking a soulmate after many years, you might be embarking on a whole new world when it comes to dating. How people meet, what they do, and how they court each other might look much different than it did when you were last hot on the scene. This can make dating seem very intimidating and possibly unappealing. But dating is not the only thing that has changed. You have changed. Your interests, likes and dislikes, social circle, stage of life—and much more—is not what it once was. That is why I recommend that you enlist your friends for support while you navigate this new world. Your friends can help you remain positive, support you when things do not go the way you planned, and they can remind you of who you are and what your values are. If your marriage ended in divorce, just make sure you don't indulge in bashing the opposite sex or talking disrespectfully about your ex. It is not productive, and it is not the vibe you want to carry with you as you look to find a partner.

Boundaries

If you self-identify as LGBTQ, you may not experience the traditional social division in genders that heterosexual folks do. Girls' night out and boys' night out may not give you the opportunity to separate from your partner—because you may be of the same sex. That is why it is so important to establish boundaries by continuing to have time with your friends without your partner. It is healthy for you to have your own lives, to feel independent, and to not be too wrapped up in each other. Be aware of your needs and make sure you continue to honor them even as your relationship develops. Enmeshing kills the sexy in a relationship and turns you into roommates eventually. Set this boundary from the start to get off on the right foot.

Don't rush into a relationship. You may bond very quickly with a new love interest and you may feel compelled to lock that down—but no matter what kind of pairing you are in, it still takes time to get to know each other. Moving too quickly is risky and often ends in disaster. You owe it to a potential long-term relationship to take your time and nurture it.

Consider the benefits of holding off on sex. Yes, you both might have a raging sex drive that makes you want to pounce ASAP, but this is not about a regular old hookup. You are looking for a relationship, and early sex confuses that goal. Sex creates a false sense of connection. That is true if you are straight, LGBTQ, polyamorous, kinky, or anything else. Sex is fun. I get it. But you are not in this for just a little fun. You are looking for a soulmate. Get to know your partner's soul before you mate. And if this is a boundary that you have set for yourself you should honor it no matter how hot he, she or they is! I promise it is worth the wait.

Needs of Others

When you are a single parent, you have the additional responsibility of caring for your little tax deductions. It is essential for you to understand that it is no longer just you and your needs that you have to consider when you begin dating. Your children's lives can be very affected by your love life. The effects can be direct, if you have brought your new partner into their lives, or indirect, because your attention and time are divided. Dividing your attention can affect your children and your new love. And kids tend to be very territorial when it comes to their parents; less time together can lead to your children feeling emotionally vulnerable.

Remember that timing is everything. Be careful of dating too soon after a breakup, death, or divorce. Your kids may still be grieving or may simply not be ready for another big change. Dating too quickly might lead your kids to be intolerant of whoever you are showing interest in and make it extremely hard for that relationship to develop in a healthy way.

In the interest of your kid's emotional well-being, you should spare them the endless parade of dates that you may go through before you find "the one." Your kids should not be a part of the process until you have a clear idea that this relationship is going somewhere. If that is unclear to you, then do your kids a favor and keep them out of it. They do not need to be aware of every person you try out. You also do not want them to get attached to someone who is not going to stick around. There are no guarantees in relationships—and you never fully know where one is headed—but you can make safer choices for your kids.

Just as with any relationship, communication is key with your children. Consider asking your kids about their thoughts about you dating when you are ready to start. When things move beyond the beginning stages, explore how they would feel if you got serious with someone you are dating. If things are serious, see if they would be down to get to know him or her. When they meet him, ask what they think about him, and so on. Allow for open communication, and keep the dialogue going. Be open to what comes up for your kids. For example, kids might find themselves in an awkward position if they like your new partner but want to remain loyal to their other parent. This might cause conflict or problematic behavior. But your communication will give you the ability to respond to them with understanding. It also provides you an opportunity to respond to your children's thoughts and feelings, and reassure or support them if that is needed.

As the relationship progresses, it will be helpful to continue to assess how your child is doing and what is in their best interest. And because you have been openly discussing the relationship, you will have a lot of information to make the best decision. You are free to date whomever you choose. That is not up to your kid. But forcing that person upon your child is unfair and can be extremely damaging.

Clearly, I believe your child's best interest is the priority. When thinking of bringing a new person into your child's life, it is extremely important for you to be mindful of the prevalence of child abuse (sexual, physical, and emotional) by stepparents. Unfortunately, it often goes unreported and children tend to keep it to themselves for fear of punishment, hurting their parent, being blamed, or experiencing shame and guilt. It is your responsibility to do your best to screen any person you are bringing in contact with your children, including a romantic interest. Speak to your children about appropriate touch and open up a dialogue with them about the subject matter so that they can come to you if they feel the slightest bit of discomfort around your new "friend."

If you are dating someone with a disability, in time, you may find your self in a caregiver role. It is natural to want to help your partner and support them when they are having difficulty or you see them struggling. You may feel guilty because you have abilities they do not. Or your might feel responsible for their happiness and well-being and make it your job to take care of their needs. But you must always remain mindful of the balance required to maintain your own self-care. Your partner's needs may seem more important than your own but they are not. You deserve to have your needs met too. Remember that you are no good to anyone if you are burned out, fatigued and neglected. Set boundaries for yourself and prioritize the things you need in your life to feel cared for and connected to the world.

Getting Your Needs Met

If you are looking for a committed relationship, it is not going to find you on your couch. Being out of the dating game due to being a single parent, getting divorced or some other reason may have gotten you out of practice. Put down the remote, change out of your sweatpants, put on something you feel good about and get out there. Socializing and mingling will help you strengthen your flirt muscles and make it possible for you to meet someone with whom you might actually be interested in flirting with. This will also help you to get out of your isolated, depressed, or angry rut where you may sit around suffering and ruminating about everything that has gone wrong in your life. Plan to do something with your downtime instead of sitting around all by yourself. It is no fun being lonely.

Dating can be fun and exciting, but it can also take some time to get back into the swing of things. Being hard on yourself when you make a mistake or are hesitant to try something will not get you anywhere. Have realistic expectations of yourself and treat yourself with kindness as you embark on this new chapter in your life. Picture yourself on a learning curve; you deserve to give yourself a pat on the back for putting forth the effort. Practice patience and understanding for yourself—and for your date too, while you are at it!

You may find yourself in a relationship with someone who comes from a family where he or she was the center of their parents' world or they may have grown up in an environment of privilege and are used to getting their needs first. This could possibly lead to you making them a priority and forgetting all about yourself. Without tuning into these subtle characteristics of your new partner you may find yourself feeling deprived, uncared for and eventually resentful. I cannot stand by and let this happen to you! Now, my advice is not to avoid only children or people who come from privilege. That would be silly. But I do think it is important for you to be clear about what your needs are before entering into a relationship and to be mindful of how your self-care practices may change once you start dating someone. If you are skipping your lunch time Yoga classes on Tuesdays and Thursdays to bring your new boo lunch, you are not living up to your responsibility to yourself. You must prioritize your own care and routinely check-in with yourself to make sure your needs are being met.

MANAGING OUTSIDE OPINIONS

People have opinions about everything! Whom you should date, how you should date them, what is appropriate to do, how to raise your potential family, and so on and so on. And the folks who are the most judgmental tend to be the most vocal about those opinions. So how can you manage the influx of opinions that may come your way when you date someone whom society (or your friends and family) may deem as unfit or wrong? It is not always easy, but it is doable. Especially when love is your guiding light.

Race is one of those issues that can make you feel as vulnerable to outside opinions as Bambi does to gunfire during hunting season. It is a touchy subject around the world and in this country, in particular. We tend to group people based on a cluster of superficial outside characteristics instead of looking at ourselves as one human race. This grouping leads to stereotypes, exclusion, racism, and unnecessary pain and suffering. Technically, race has nothing to do with biology. It is a social construct, created by people based on nothing more than appearance. Genetically, our make-up crosses racial lines and is shared among all racial classifications. But I digress! Because race is a touchy subject at large, there are definitely strong opinions about what some may call "interracial dating."

In much of Brooklyn, especially where I live, interracial dating is quite normal. Families are often a blend of race, ethnicity, culture, faith, nationality, socioeconomic status, educational background, and more. This trend is on the rise in much of the country. There is a definite shift in the way our society views interracial coupling. It was less than fifty years ago that the US Supreme Court decision Loving v. Virginia led to the removal of the miscegenation laws present in the remaining sixteen states to uphold them. Yes, there was an actual law banning people from marrying outside of their race that led to real jail time if you were convicted! Since then, interracial dating has steadily been on the rise and is much more accepted today. However, the mere fact that I have had to write that previous sentence denotes there are still those who will not only give a multiethnic couple the side eye but will also discriminate against them and treat them with disdain and hatred. So, although the choice to date whomever you like despite racial differences is not as controversial as it once was, this does not mean there won't be challenges along the way.

When my husband, Brian, and I first started dating, we were often met with smiles. People would stop us and tell us what a beautiful couple we were. We were in New York City and our melting pot community was very accepting of us. Brian was not the first man I had dated outside of my racial and cultural background, but he was the one I felt most connected to and comfortable around, and that showed for both of us. My dating philosophy was always an open one. If you were nice and if I was even slightly attracted to you, I would give you a chance. That led me to a rich dating experience with guys who shared similarities to my ethnic background and those who were much different from what I knew. It wasn't until I started dating Brian though, that I became very serious with anyone. He was my first long-term partner. As we became more serious, we were met with concerns or unsolicited statements from people inside of our families. I remember very clearly standing outside by the BBQ with one of my husband's family members and being asked if people stared at us because we were different, the implication being that we were abnormal and somehow unacceptable by others. Spending time with members of the older generations in his family was often uncomfortable initially because they were not onboard with our relationship and did not know how to engage with me even though I was "one of the good ones," according to them. (Cue the eye roll!) I had a very close family member of my own share that one of her "friends" told her that I was "the whole package: smart, talented, beautiful, accomplished, and personable, EXCEPT I wasn't with a black guy." She not only shared this thought but seemed to endorse it! And there have been many more microaggressions from others we have experienced throughout our relationship, though I am happy to say we have developed strong connections with each other's families based on love and respect over the years.

These experiences, though hurtful, were somewhat anticipated. Even though we were quite young, we were not stupid. The "post-racial society" that has been pushed on us in recent years does not exist now and it certainly didn't exist then. That is why it is important to expect that there may be those who are close to you who disapprove of your relationship just because you do not look like your partner. Be prepared to respond to their objections thoughtfully instead of defensively. Know that, even as you might interpret their resistance as ignorant, racist, and misguided, they are most likely coming from a place of concern and, ironically, love. I say most likely because I am very aware that sometimes the resistance will simply be ignorant, racist, and misguided. In that case, I share a sigh of exasperation with you and encourage you to persevere in the face of ugliness.

> " ... it is important to expect that there may be those who are close to you that disapprove of your relationship just because you do not look like your partner."

As a couple, you two will be met with all kinds of challenges. Just like any other challenge, this one should be discussed. Disapproval from others will not just be about racism, social status, or the fact that you guys do not look alike. It can also be about a fear that you will abandon your culture. Be willing to talk about how your relationship is not a threat to your family's cultural background and how you plan on sharing your cultures and honoring each other's heritage. Your relationship can be a celebration of your diverse backgrounds instead of a battle between the two of you about who has the better cultural practices. You have the opportunity to learn about each other and share your experiences of food, music, practices, holidays, rituals, and more. This cooperative nature will come in handy if there is friction between your families regarding your cultures. If you two can come up with a collaborative strategy about how to handle pushback from your loved ones, you will come out of each situation stronger and more connected.

If someone is unwilling to be open to your relationship, there is nothing you can do about that. However, most people who disapprove or share concern will learn the error of their ways over time as they become a witness to the beautiful, loving, and healthy relationship you have. You are in this relationship for yourselves and not for anybody else. If the two of you are happy and feel good about what you have, let that be the guiding force behind your growth as a couple. Let your awareness of what other people are bringing to the table and what their motives may be inform you instead of making you reactive. If you approach this problem from a mindful place you will be able to let go of your judgments of others and come to a place of resolve within yourself and perhaps with others. There are many relationships that seem to have it all from the outside and meet their families' standards of what a relationship should be and they still fail. The motivation behind your relationship lasting must always be internal. External validation has never been the key to partner bliss.

Religion or faith is another hot issue that can bring about a lot of outside opinions. Religion has been the basis of many conflicts. Wars have been waged, cities have been divided, and people have been marginalized, judged, and at times, persecuted. Romantic relationships are certainly not immune to the perils of such conflicts. But most religions have one thing in common: an underlying theme of love. Religion does not have to be a relationship deal breaker. Believe it or not, your differences might even bring you closer to your partner and yourself.

You are attracted to your partner for a reason. What they present on the outside might have brought you together initially, but it is most likely whom they are that has kept your interest. If your partner has strong religious convictions that seem to conflict with your own, you might view this as a threat to your relationship. However, their faith is a part of what makes them attractive to you because it is part of who they are. You must get to know your partner's religious beliefs before dismissing them. It is ignorant to make assumptions based on what you think without getting to know the facts. Your partner could be unwavering in their faith and demand that you be the same. There may be aspects that are more cultural than religious. Perhaps they want their religious practices to be a part of their family, but are open to incorporating other practices as well. Take the time to learn about their beliefs and expose yourself to their ceremonies, rituals, and prayers. Do so with an open heart and mind. Let love be the motivation. You might even find that you like some of your partner's practices and are more receptive to them than you had anticipated. Your interest in all parts of your partner, including their spiritual background, will give you are clearer picture of who you are as a couple and where the potential lies.

Compromise is often highlighted as one of the key ingredients to a successful relationship. You will have to make many compromises and sacrifices to keep a happy balance in a partnership. The same is true of your partner. But does that mean that you have to change what you believe in to make a relationship work? Absolutely not! I want to be very clear that you can have different religious views and still be respectful of your partner's beliefs. You may have to experiment with your partner to figure out how to make this work but you can make it work. As a kid and adult, I have happily attended Catholic, Jewish, and nonreligious spiritual services and never felt my Christian beliefs or friendships were threatened. I attend services at the Oriental Mission Church in Los Angeles several times and never once felt like my ethnic identity was unsafe among the Korean congregation. I felt closer to my friends, getting to know them in such an intimate way. Through those experiences, I got to know more about what was important to me. Heck, I even dated a guy my freshman year of college who was on track to become a pastor at a megachurch in Southern California. I mean, I considered myself to be Christian because that was how I was raised, but it was not until that relationship that I became aware of the many differences between Christian beliefs depending on which congregation you were part of. It helped me to get a better understanding of where I stood spiritually. It was because of those events that I could be respectful of my husband's spiritual beliefs and be open to his challenges with religion without feeling like I had to join him in his exact ideology. Nor do I feel compelled to convert him to my beliefs and practices. This may be more challenging for others because of less exposure to different religions and strong faith and cultural ties, but you can learn to honor your partner and their beliefs while still holding your own beliefs close to heart.

If you come from a family with strong religious ties and values, you might have an additional obstacle. They may be resistant to your partnership and feel their values are endangered. Most people want their partners to be accepted by their families immediately. It sure does make things more comfortable to be welcomed with open arms into another family. But we cannot always control this. Make sure you and your partner have a strong connection before putting them in this environment and discuss the possibility that they may not be accepted initially. The two of you can figure out how to manage this while being supportive and respectful of each other.

Coming from different religious backgrounds can be hard to navigate in a relationship. But it doesn't have to be a deal breaker. In fact, you have the advantage of discussing the way you envision your family, how to raise your kids, what holidays you find important to observe, and what practices you want to share. A lot of couples go into long-term relationships without discussing any of these things and find that they are at an impasse years into their families that could have been avoided if they had explored these values earlier on.

Look at your religious differences as an asset to your relationship instead of as a liability. Learn to respect each other's beliefs, be open to what your partner is bringing to the table, share your history and practices, and collaborate with each other. You can do so without giving up anything. Instead you can add richness to your spiritual life and your relationship.

As we can see there are many combinations of backgrounds, identities, and make-ups that can impact how we date. A mindful presence can allow you to open up to those unique qualities you each bring to the relationship and give you the opportunity to incorporate, honor and love the parts of yourself and of your mate that make them distinct from you. Keep honesty, navigating needs, and managing outside opinions in mind as you go through this book and begin to incorporate these new tools and practices. Think of your individuality and uniqueness as an asset not a handicap. Your differences do not have to separate you. They can bring you closer together. Your circumstances do not have to disqualify you. They can make you a stronger partner. Your identity does not have to be threatening to the potential of forming a loving and lasting bond with a life partner. Embrace who you are and be willing to do the same for the one you love.

PART TWO
THE PRINCIPLES OF MINDFUL DATING

4 DATING IN THE MOMENT

Charlotte is a twenty-four-year-old African American lesbian woman who has been in therapy on-and-off since she was a teenager. As an actress, she is trained to access her emotions very easily, and she was not shy to express herself when we first met. She has a flair for the dramatic—she is quite entertaining and very likable. When Charlotte was a freshman in college she was sexually assaulted by her then-boyfriend after a small party they threw for a few friends. He and his friends were drinking, and after everyone had left, he wanted to take their unconsummated relationship to the next level. When she expressed reservations about having intercourse he disregarded her feelings, told her she would like it, and forced himself on her. Feeling somewhat responsible for what happened, she never reported the incident and did not tell anyone about it. She acted as if it never happened and eventually broke off the relationship.

A year or two later Charlotte came out as lesbian and began casually dating women, but she was not ready for a committed relationship. However, recently she met a woman whom she is very attracted to. They have been on a few dates and are just getting to know each other, but so far she likes what she sees in Lisa. Except for one thing that came up on their last date: Lisa showed up fifteen minutes late due to being held up at an after-work event. Lisa texted Charlotte to say she got held up and was on her way. She finally arrived, but it was later than the agreed-upon time. This may not have been a big deal if Lisa had not also been drinking. As soon as Charlotte recognized that Lisa had had a couple glasses of wine at her event, she became anxious. She was uncomfortable being with Lisa and felt agitated. Though unaware of them at the time, she had thoughts about how Lisa must not care about her and how she had proven herself to be untrustworthy. She imagined this would probably lead to her being hurt or victimized in some way. When Lisa attempted to explain the situation and apologize, Charlotte wanted nothing to do with it and pushed Lisa away—both emotionally and physically when Lisa tried to touch her hand.

In session, Charlotte was in tears because she had been so hopeful about the relationship until the last date. Since then she had not responded to Lisa's texts or calls as she had decided that things couldn't work between the two of them. We explored in what way Lisa's behavior was indicative of her being untrustworthy, and it was difficult for Charlotte to put it into words. Eventually, she admitted the fact that Lisa was drinking was all the proof she needed that Lisa was not to be trusted. Charlotte had been sexually assaulted by her ex when he was drunk, and Lisa's drinking triggered fear in her. I helped Charlotte to see that what her ex did to her was wrong and horrible ... but that not all people who drink sexually assault others. Charlotte was also able to see that Lisa was not drunk, that she had communicated with her about the event, and that she was running behind. She could admit that she had been viewing Lisa through the same lens as she saw her ex—even though they, and the circumstances, were very different.

"Dating in the moment means being present in your mind, body, and spirit while you are out with someone."

Dating in the moment means being present in your mind, body, and spirit while you are out with someone. When we have had difficult past experiences it can be a challenge to stay in the moment. But it is not necessary for us to have had a past trauma for us to find ourselves on automatic pilot on a date. Discomfort, insecurity, worry, fear, anxiety, judgmental thoughts, and more can influence whether we remain in the now. When we are not present, we are not connecting with the person we are with. When we are out of the present moment and into a past or imagined future moment, we become reactive to the person we are with instead of responsive. Charlotte's case is an extreme example of how unresolved past experiences may impact the way we are able to interact with a good potential partner. In her case, the traumatic assault she experienced prevented her from being present on her date with Lisa because she overgeneralized Lisa's drinking to mean that she was a threat just like her ex. She was not with Lisa in the moment—she was with her ex.

There is much to be gained from learning to date in the moment. In this chapter we will explore exactly what can be achieved through mindful dating. Yes, you know by now why mindfulness can be helpful, but let's look at how it can transform your dating life.

A GREATER SENSE OF REALITY

Imagine being out on a date and really being there. I don't just mean physically there, I mean you are present in every way. You are connected to where you are and who you are with. You are aware of how you are feeling and what you are thinking. You are taking in the here and now without prejudging it, without letting past experiences taint it—and you are able to be yourself. This is the essence of dating in the moment.

When we are able to interact with the person we are with in the present moment—just as it is—we are able to truly connect with them in all ways possible. Dating is a total-body experience. So if part of us is not there, how can it be successful? Our minds have to be there with us to avoid superficial interactions. We have to be spiritually grounded, and compatible in our behaviors and values. And of course we have to be physically present, or we leave ourselves vulnerable to being out of touch with reality.

As you have probably gathered by now, I am a bit of a pop culture fanatic. I love television, movies, Broadway, red carpet events, concerts, celebrity weddings, and so on. I have a longstanding relationship with these sources of entertainment. But many things are not constant when it comes to pop culture. Marriages dissolve, comedy shows are cancelled, and Broadway shows close. However, in my life there has been one ever-present constant, since the day I was born until now: *The Young and the Restless*. Those of us who know the joy of escaping into Genoa City and the lives of the Newmans, Abbots, and Winters know there is comfort in the show's dependability. It is always there. However, this can be a bit of an issue when you get caught up in a compelling, though often deliciously ridiculous, storyline. I have been known to get so involved that I start talking to the screen. "Sharon, you better wise up and realize your best friend, Grace, is sleeping with your husband, Nick!" (This may or may not have been something that I yelled to the television at one of those moments.) I have gotten so caught up in the plot that the line separating real life from the soap opera has become blurred. Luckily, it becomes clear to me shortly after such outbursts that Sharon, Grace, and Nick are not real. It is not always that easy when it comes to what is going on in our minds.

When we are unaware of how our mind is at work, we can let our thoughts run away with us. Like a ball of snow gaining more mass and momentum as it rolls down a mountain, more thoughts, ideas, and images are generated as we become more involved in our made-up storyline. We actively participate in the series of events that happen in our minds and get swept away by a plot that is not necessarily real. Because they are so developed, these ideas are able to capture and grab hold of our attention. The thoughts are taken as factual, and we buy into them. The strong and influential images thrust you into an action state where you become reactive to them. And there you are, out of step with what is actually happening.

Losing sight of what is true happens to all of us, believe me, but without awareness you are more likely to engage in this cycle more often. You can be especially vulnerable to doing this while you are on a date because dating can trigger all kinds of feelings, memories, thoughts, and behaviors. All it takes is one intrusive thought to create a narrative so believable that it will distract you from the real situation. These thoughts keep you from your intended goal of connecting with someone new and seeing if there may be something there to explore. With a greater sense of reality, you begin to see what is actually there—good or bad—instead of being led by what you're imagining.

FLEXIBILITY AND SPACIOUSNESS

"Few minds are spacious; few even have an empty place in them or can offer some vacant point. Almost all have narrow capacities and are filled by some knowledge that blocks them up. What a torture to talk to filled heads, that allow nothing from the outside to enter them! A good mind, in order to enjoy itself and allow itself to enjoy others, always keeps itself larger than its own thoughts. In order to do this, these thoughts must be given a pliant form, must be easily folded and unfolded, so that they are capable, finally, of maintaining a natural flexibility."

—Joseph Joubert, *The Notebooks of Joseph Joubert*

We have thousands of thoughts going through our minds at all times. All this activity makes it difficult to make room for new thoughts and ideas. Unfortunately, this can cause us to get stuck on the same thought loop over and over again. We hold on to to old beliefs and prevent fresh ones from coming in. When it comes to dating, a stuffed and rigid mind can stop a love connection dead in its tracks. A suitor has no chance if you have beliefs that are so strong that they cannot be challenged. As soon as your date does something that contradicts what you "know" to be true, the trajectory of your relationship changes. Now, this may be appropriate in some cases. Say you are on a date and the guy texts others all night, stares at your boobs the entire time, hits on the hostess, and treats the waitress like a peon. Well, that's a clear indication that he is not ready for a committed relationship—or the affection of another human being for that matter. But if you have a rigid belief that the person you are dating should maintain eye contact with you at all times while you are together to show that he is into you, and he falls short of that expectation ... are you likely to take into account that he expressed genuine interest in you, asked a lot of great questions, had a lot in common with you, and was a gentleman? Probably not. Those beliefs will probably stop you from looking for an alternate explanation, such as the possibility that he might be shy or insecure. For there to be a chance for new ideas to be explored, there has to be space in your mind and around your thoughts. For positive change to happen in your life you have to learn to be flexible in your views so that the truth can be revealed.

"When it comes to dating, a stuffed and rigid mind can stop a love connection dead in its tracks."

When most people think of being flexible, they think about their bodies, but we are talking about a different kind of flexibility. Mental flexibility describes the ability to shift between two cognitive processes and to be able to think of multiple ideas at the same time. Basically, this means you can consider more than one possibility and switch between ideas to come up with a belief that is all-encompassing. A flexible mind is an open mind. And an open mind is unrestricted and unlimited. We develop a rigid mindset as way to protect ourselves and simplify things. It is a defensive action that gives us quick results and seems effective ... but in reality it keeps us from being good problem solvers and hinders our creativity, mental agility, and positivity. The costs clearly outweigh the benefits here. Learning to identify and then let go of rigid beliefs can be challenging, but the hard work certainly pays off in the end.

"A flexible mind is an open mind. And an open mind is unrestricted and unlimited."

Spaciousness in the mind refers to the expansion of the mind through awareness and non-judgment. Your thoughts exist, but they do not fill your mind. You are aware of them, but instead of holding on to them tightly, you observe them without judgment and allow them to come and go as they will. Imagine your dream closet with different sections, custom shoe racks, built-in drawers, beautiful lighting, and a sitting area. It is tailored to your specific needs and preferences, and in that closet you have some of the most amazing bags, shoes, jewelry, and outfits. However, the closet is also filled to the brim with countless bags full of clothes you cannot let go of. It is so stuffed that you can't even close the door, let alone find your amazing Jimmy Choos. So you end up wearing the same tired old clothes that you have been wearing because you do not have access to your amazing wardrobe. This is your beautiful mind without spaciousness. You may have a lot of great thoughts, but they are hidden underneath a bunk of junk thoughts that you are hoarding—and there is no room for fabulous new thoughts to enter or exit. Just as you need to create room in your closet for new clothes and see what items to keep and what items to donate or throw in the garbage, you need to create room in your mind for new thoughts to come in and for old thoughts to be observed, evaluated, and discarded if they are no longer useful. This kind of spaciousness of mind allows your problems to exist without letting them control you, because of the clarity and broadening of your perspective that develops.

Flexibility and spaciousness work together to create a mind that is unburdened and free to explore multiple ideas and accept alternate explanations. It is a gift to be able to let go of our need to know everything and have an answer to all of our problems before they even occur. It gives you the chance to open up to all things possible, increasing your opportunities for joy, pleasure, and connectivity.

FREEING YOURSELF FROM THE WEB OF PROBLEMS, INSECURITIES, AND WORRIES

The practice of mindfulness makes it possible for us to decide how we want to respond to a situation. Instead of tuning out on a date and letting our minds wander, awareness offers us a way to stay tuned into what is happening around us. When we are being reactive to a problem, we can recognize habitual ways of thinking or behaving. We have the opportunity to assess what our values are, and to decide whether or not our choices are in line with those values. We can decide how we want to engage with a situation. We restore our power to be our genuine selves.

I often hear people tell me when discussing their behaviors and actions that they did not have a choice; things "just happened." That it was like an out-of-body experience. But this is not true. We may have strong emotions that seem to overcome us—or we may be guided by rigid beliefs that make us reactive to a situation— but there is always a choice. It is when we discover that we are capable of choosing how we behave and what we believe that our truest potential for self-realization develops. With self-realization comes potential for growth in all areas of our lives, including in our romantic relationships.

See how dating in the moment can really change the dating game? As you begin to practice mindfulness you will see that the benefits are real and powerful. Dating does not have to be distressing. Through more awareness, spaciousness, and flexibility of the mind, a greater sense reality, and freedom from our worries, we are better equipped to handle a bad date or two without losing sight of who we are, what is important to us, and how we can achieve a sense of contentment even when things are not going our way. Additionally, you will be more likely to pick up on whether or not you are with a dud or a stud—and to prevent yourself from pushing good candidates away. And because you are more dialed into who you are, you will probably attract partners and friends alike who are more suitable

5 USING YOUR BREATH

You have known how to breathe since the day you were born. You do it every day and usually do not give it a second thought. That is ... until something happens to trigger a response in you that changes your breathing. It can be anything from walking up four flights of stairs, to seeing your ex-college crush in a television promo ad for the NBC drama *Chicago Med*. I know when my husband gives me that sexy "you look like a delicious pork chop I am ready to sop up in gravy" gaze, I always feel breathless. Okay, these examples were very specific to my experiences, so feel free to substitute your own breathtaking events. It is not until something happens that changes our normal breathing pattern that we take notice of our breath and how it can affect us. Intentionally bringing awareness to your breath can be calming and stabilizing; it can reduce stress and anxiety, and help you to get in touch with what is happening in your mind and in your body. Let's take a closer look at the benefits of being aware of your breath.

"Intentionally bringing awareness to your breath can be calming and stabilizing; it can reduce stress and anxiety and help you to get in touch with what is happening in your mind and in your body."

Many meditation exercises use mindful breathing as the basis for the practice because of how readily available the breath always is to you. You can try to focus on your breath, and as you attempt to do so, you will also become aware of something else: boy, can your mind wander! Your mind is able to leap from a grocery list to that broken toenail you forgot to file, all in a single bound. But it is not done there. If you are unaware, your mind can continue to wander from one thing to another indefinitely. Mindful breathing is done in a nonjudgmental way, allowing those thoughts to pop in and out of our minds without trying to change them and without becoming involved with them or attached to them. Nonjudgmental thinking means that we have a thought, accept that thought for what it is, do not criticize it or do anything with it, and let it pass.

Here's the secret: thoughts will pass. If you learn to let go of them, they will come and go like the summer vacationers who visit the Jersey Shore. The more you practice doing this with meditation, the more you will be able to do it in your day-to-day life!

ADVANTAGES

There is lots of talk in mindfulness about "doing" and "being." We are a culture of doers. We value doers and what they can accomplish over who they are as a person. We usually do not praise people for sitting in silence and simply being with themselves. However, anyone who has ever tried to sit in silence will tell you it is a skill that has to be developed, and it does not come easily for most us. As a chronic doer myself, it took a lot of time before I was even willing to try just being. *Who has time for that?* I used to think. However, when my life was starting to become unmanageable due to all the tasks I was juggling, I realized that I had no balance. I was all "doing" and no "being." There was no room in my life to sit with my own thoughts, to be curious about how I was feeling, or to relax. I was on a speeding train headed for BurnOutVille, and I was ready to get off. The goal for me was not to stop doing, but to balance things out by prioritizing moments of being. Mindful breathing is a wonderful way to anchor yourself to the present moment and take a break from doing.

Anxiety and dating go hand and hand. It can be difficult to stop yourself from thinking about what can come from a good or bad connection with someone new. You may find yourself imagining where you will live and what your children will look like before you have even met the guy in person. Or your anxiety can keep you from being yourself because you are worried about how things may go, what you might say, if he will think you are attractive, or if he is good enough for you. Anxiety is all about worrying about the future. It is fear, worry, or concern about what could or could not happen. When we ruminate or think excessively about our anxious thoughts, we start to make those thoughts our reality, and then we react to them. Mindful breathing helps us to get back into the here and the now by focusing on what is happening around and within in us. Doing this interrupts the ruminative thoughts, thus creating a more relaxed and clear mind. It shifts our focus from one thing (worrying about the future) to another (the rhythm of our breath). If your mind is not focused on your fictional thoughts, then your anxiety decreases and your mind becomes more calm and restful.

Try this on for size: research has shown that mindful breathing can not only improve mental states but can also benefit your physical health. This tool is used to help cancer patients manage the harmful side effects that may be present with certain treatments. It is effective in helping to fight obesity. It improves the nervous system and the quality of the blood. It can strengthen your heart, lungs, muscles, and immune system. It aids in the relief of pain and can lower your blood pressure. This is just a glimpse into how it can improve your overall physical health. Approaching life with a healthy mind and body will bring about more favorable outcomes—and when less favorable ones present themselves, you will be equipped to handle it.

CHALLENGES

As amazing as mindful breathing may sound, there are challenges to doing it. One pretty common challenge I hear about often is quite simple: "I didn't feel like doing it." The "I don't want to" mentality is quite prevalent in our society. In the information age, where technology puts everything at our fingertips, we have become very good at not having to if we do not want to. Don't want to cook? We have Seamless, GrubHub, and other food delivery services to take care of it. Don't want to drive? Call an Uber or a Lyft. Don't want to go shopping? Sit on your couch with a bag of Buffalo Hot Wing Pretzel Bits in one hand and search RueLaLa, ShopBop, BlueFly or any of the many online boutiques with the other. So what happens if we do not feel like being in the moment? We tune out. We stay on autopilot. We give in to the tendency to stay disconnected. Who can blame you? Being in the present moment can seem unpleasant if things are not the way we want them to be. Sometimes the here and now is the last place you want to be. So you give into the urge to avoid. It is the easiest thing to do. So your mind wanders, and you avoid the present moment— only to find that time has gone by but your problems remain the same or have gotten worse. You have done what you have set out to do without even thinking about it, but the results are fleeting and ineffective in the long run.

For this pattern to change, you must first notice how it exists in your life and accept that it is not helping you. This very important first step puts you in the position to do something about it. Slowing down the rapid-fire thoughts of the mind can be just as difficult as getting a very active toddler to settle down. However, with consistent training you can begin to get a handle on your thoughts. Good mental health—like good physical health— requires training. With improved mental fitness, you can be alert to when you are distracted and then make a choice about how you want to attend to the moment.

Perhaps you are actively avoiding practicing a new skill like mindful breathing, or perhaps you lack motivation. One of the most common symptoms of depression is a lack of motivation. However, you do not have to be clinically depressed to experience a lack of motivation from time to time. I have noticed that there is a tendency for people to be very hard on themselves when they lack drive. People expect to feel motivated before they take action. When they don't, they criticize themselves for being lazy. But that is an unhelpful way of thinking about your drive. Waiting to feel motivated can keep you stagnant for way too long. One of my favorite things to tell my clients is that action comes before motivation. You might not feel like doing it, but it is doing it that will make you feel like doing it again. By gently pushing yourself to act even when you feel unmotivated, you create a new pattern of behavior. It is your intention to practice that becomes your drive. To really practice mindfulness, it will be your intention—not force—that gets you into the present moment. As you build this skill and start to reap the benefits, eventually you will recognize that you are feeling more and more motivated to do what you have been less inclined to do for yourself.

"Action comes before motivation."

Other challenges include being overscheduled, not buying into the idea of mindful breathing, not having the "right" place to do it, and a host of other excuses. Just like anything that is important to you, you have to prioritize it. We all have very busy lives. I know I tend to sit and think about all of my duties as a mother, wife, business owner, professional, friend, daughter, sister, and so on, and I can get very overwhelmed. It took me a very long time to give mindfulness a chance. But when I started with mindful breathing, it became clear to me that this tool was the most important gift I could give to myself. It gave me the awareness to know how to approach my life in much healthier way. I do not always get things right, but I sure do feel better about the choices I make and am better able to handle and learn from my mistakes.

Strategies

Cyclical Breathing

I find it is best to identify a quiet place to sit and practice this skill, but it is certainly not necessary. I have practiced cyclical breathing while standing on the train, in a quiet spot, or in the middle of a disastrous Thanksgiving family conflict. However, while you are learning, try to find a quiet, relaxing spot in your house, in the park, in your car, or in the office bathroom. In my experience, as little as three minutes of mindful breathing can give you positive results. This may sound like only a short amount of time, but trust me, three minutes can seem like an eternity. At the beginning of building this skill I recommend you start with only a few minutes and then increase the time when you feel you have mastered it.

This exercise is quite simple. Set your timer for three minutes. Sit up in an erect and fully alert position. Breathe in through your nose and breathe out through your mouth. While breathing in through your nose, count 1-2-3 and notice the pause after you inhale. Then breathe out through your mouth, count 1-2-3 and notice the pause after you exhale. Repeat until your timer goes off.

As you can see, the exercise is a repeated cycle of inhales and exhales. It can be helpful to think of the cycle as a circle where you inhale at the top of the circle and exhale at the bottom of the circle.

When you breathe, try not to control the breath. Use the counting as a guide to steady your breathing, but do not force it. There will be many things to pay attention to while you practice. You may notice there is a natural pause in between your inhale and exhale. You may notice the rise and fall of your chest. You may notice how your breath feels (in the form of sensation or warmth) going in your nose or coming out of your mouth. Use this as a way to pay attention to what is happening now.

Your mind will wander ... a lot. That's okay. That is what a mind does. Notice what you are thinking about, and gently refocus yourself on your breathing. If you are able to do this just one time then the exercise was a success! And remember this is a skill you are developing, and you will get better at it with practice. Start by practicing twice a day, perhaps once in the morning when you wake up and once in the evening before getting ready to go to bed.

A Mindful Breath

Sometimes all we have is a moment. In those times, a quick exercise may be in order. A mindful breath requires you to stop whatever it is that you are doing and close your eyes. Take one full single breath in through your nose and out through your mouth.

Notice if you lose focus, and refocus by trying again, if needed. Now, ask yourself: *What am I thinking, what am I feeling, and what is happening in my body?* Be open to whatever comes to the surface. Take a pause before you act, and pay attention to your breathing again for a few breaths. Reenter the room by opening your eyes, and respond to what is happening around you with the information you were just able to access.

Comfort Breathing

Many years ago I took a yoga and anxiety training in Staten Island, New York, with Mary NurrieStearns, the coauthor with her husband, Rick, of *Yoga for Anxiety: Meditations and Practices for Calming the Body and Mind.* In this training she introduced me to "the comfort pose." Since then I have regularly incorporated it into my business practice and personal practice.

You can either sit erect or lie down. Take your right hand and place it over your heart. Then take your left hand and wrap it around your waist, holding on to the right side of your waist. Relax your chest and your belly. Breathe in through your nose deeply and slowly. Breathe out slowly through your mouth.

Feel the warmth of your hands on your body. Feel where your hands and your body connect. Feel your loving embrace. Feel how your hands rise and fall with your belly and chest. This breathing exercise is warm, gentle, loving, and very comforting. You can do it anywhere and commit to as little as one minute or as long as you need. When your mind wanders, pay attention to what you are thinking about and then gently refocus yourself on comfort breathing.

Mindful breathing is the foundation of a majority of mindfulness exercises for a very important reason. It is the easiest and most effective way to get in touch with what is happening in the present moment. Using your breath is great place to start your mindfulness practice. The strategies above are simple yet effective. Use them as indicated and see how they can benefit you and your dating experience.

6 GETTING ACQUAINTED WITH YOUR THOUGHTS

I've been dating since I was fifteen.
I'm exhausted. Where is he?
—*Charlotte York*

Dating can be pretty stressful even for the most confident of us. You have to be vulnerable, get out of your comfort zone, put yourself out there—and there is always the possibility you will be rejected. Why do we do this to ourselves again? Oh, that's right! It is because the possibility of finding someone you truly connect with is worth the risk. Fear, insecurity, and worry may start to pop up, and that is understandable under the circumstances. We all have negative thoughts to some degree. It is when these negative thoughts get out of control, affect our functioning, or prevent us from progressing that we need to make some serious changes. I like to call this undertaking Mission Cognition.

"Mission Cognition is the operation of becoming more familiar with our warped thoughts."

Mission Cognition is the operation of becoming more familiar with our warped thoughts. Cognitive distortions are common around dating. Mention of these hot thoughts were first introduced to us by Cognitive Behavioral Therapy pioneer, Dr. Aaron

Beck and later clearly packaged for us by CBT heavyweight Judith Beck, PhD, in her classic book *Cognitive Behavioral Therapy: Basics and Beyond*. She shows us how negative thoughts can play a significant role in our mood and behavior. When you have a bad experience, heartbreak, or disappointment, you might get a little (or a lot) confused about dating and how the process is "supposed" to work. This happens to the best of us and is not an indication of our level of intelligence. For example, I have worked with doctors, lawyers, teachers, and college professors who have had warped thoughts about dating. This kind of stinking thinking can lead to self-defeating behaviors and can flat out ruin a date or relationship before it gets off the ground.

Another fact about warped thoughts: the more you overthink or excessively go over a negative idea, thought, or worry, the more likely it will become a part of your narrative. What this means is that over time, the familiarity your mind develops with your distorted thoughts fosters the belief that the distortions are true. This is only natural. Eventually, the thoughts become automatic and are part of the way we see ourselves, others, and the world. It is like the repeated coverage and praise of the college football sensation Johnny Manziel. We all believed the hype. He was supposed to be God's gift to football—and he did have a lot of potential. However, the coverage of Johnny Football left out that our beloved new NFL quarterback had a lot of maturing to do. Partying and bad behavior soon became the story. We did not have the whole picture, but because we were constantly being fed certain pieces of information, we bought into it. Our own ruminative thoughts can play in our minds like the always-airing program *Sports Center* on ESPN, and they can be pretty influential in what we believe.

Now that we have formed these distorted thoughts about dating, we are at risk. By repeatedly telling yourself the same thing, these ideas can become deeply rooted in you. Your thoughts become more automatic and are triggered when you are dating or thinking about dating. Once you wholeheartedly believe in the distorted thought, it can begin to take control of your behavior. You might start avoiding dating, or become overly prepared for each date. You may decide the best defense is a great offense—or you could tell yourself not to defend yourself against offensive behavior. Like ideas, the behaviors can become fixed and can prevent you from moving forward and reaching your dating goals. By becoming aware of these destructive thoughts, you can stop the negative emotions associated with them from taking over—and you can learn to identify, challenge, and modify them.

Dr. Judith Beck identified the many different ways our minds can twist our thoughts. Considering the work she has done on this subject, I have put together a list of some of the more common thinking distortions around dating. As you read over it, be mindful of what seems familiar, and feel free to put a check mark next to the ones you can identify with.

DATING DISTORTIONS

Common Dating Distortions include:
- Mind reading
- Should statements
- Black or white thinking
- Catastrophizing
- Discounting the positives
- Overgeneralization
- Emotional reasoning
- Personalizing
- What if-ing
- Labeling and judging

Mind Reading

Mind reading is what you do when you tell yourself that you know just what someone else is thinking and feeling—and why they are acting and reacting the way they are without having any real proof. The thoughts tend to be negative assumptions that you buy into, without considering other possibilities.

I have been the mind reader many times in my life. I can tell you, there is nothing more frustrating than having someone deny the thoughts in their mind that you have clearly uncovered. Wait a second ... something doesn't sound right here. Oh yeah, *I can't read minds.* It may be equally or even just a little more infuriating to be told by someone else what you are thinking when you know it is not the truth—unless you're like my daughter who marvels at my ability to know just what she is thinking (through mother's intuition, context clues, and body language, of course). I cannot read your mind, and you cannot read mine—or anybody else's.

Should Statements

We constantly "should" ourselves throughout the day. From taking the stairs up six flights to doing the dishes, there are a lot of decisions to be made. Over time these ideas you have created can become a rigid and precise list of rules that are unbreakable and "should" be met. If the rules are broken, then you get disappointed or angry at yourself. Or you might feel guilty or resentful because your expectations have not been met. Basically, "should" statements are fixed beliefs that serve as a way to criticize yourself or others, and these statements limit your experiences and possibilities.

Dating can be a regular "should" statement breeding ground. I hear it all the time. He should have a full head of hair for me to be into him. I should feel instant chemistry with him if we are meant to be. He should have taken me to the four-star restaurant downtown instead of Shake Shack. With so many conditions you are likely to "should yourself" out of a love life. Now, we all deserve to have standards that we uphold. However, if your list of "shoulds" outweighs the number of successful dates you have had, then it is probably a good time to investigate your beliefs and switch it up a bit. Don't be fooled by a tricky "should" statement. Sometimes a "should" is disguised as a "must," "have to," or "oughta." It is all the same.

Black and White Thinking

Some people tend to live in extremes. Things are either good or bad, wrong or right, helpful or unhelpful, etc. However, most of us do not live in a polarized world like the one portrayed in *Star Wars*. It was very clear that the Empire and the Dark Side were evil, tyrannous, unforgiving, and callous enough about life that they could blow up a planet full of beings just because they felt like it. It was equally easy to see that the Jedi were pure, righteous, and good. Here in the real world, things are usually not so black and white.

Black-or-white thinking is what you do when you see things in terms of all or nothing. There is no middle ground. There is no other point on the spectrum that can be identified as a reasonable alternative to your binary thoughts. You are on one side of the pole or the other. As a result, if you fall short of perfection you see it as a total failure. For example, *I completely ruined the date when I didn't know enough about hockey to show interest.* If you go into dating with this type of thinking, you will constantly feel rejected, unsatisfied, and unsuccessful. Why? Because things are rarely black or white. There is good to be found in bad and bad to be found in good.

Catastrophizing

Catastrophic thoughts can be overwhelming and panic-inducing. Now just imagine what it must be like to have catastrophic thoughts regularly. Some do not have to wonder about this because it is their reality. Remember the twenty-four-year-old actress, Charlotte, whom we discussed earlier? She is bombarded by these types of thoughts. One morning, she sat on my couch in a frenzy because she realized that she did not have her phone when she got on the train to come to session. I must admit, I feel a slight wave of panic at the thought of not having my phone, as do many of us. We are very attached to our smart devices, and it is hard to remember how we got along without them. However, for Charlotte the panic was more than a slight wave. She imagined that while she was without her phone, her successful, well-established adult brother would have an accident and would need her help. Because she did not have her phone, he would not have a means of contacting her; he would sit in a ditch in pain and be susceptible to thugs on the street who would take advantage of his inability to defend himself. To Charlotte this catastrophic prediction felt real and likely to occur.

Catastrophic thinking is what you do when you focus on the worst possible outcome of a situation. This might happen to anyone at times, but most of us are able to talk ourselves down from the ledge by looking at the big picture. Someone with chronic catastrophic thoughts exaggerates the significance of things and then blows them way out of proportion. Can you imagine what this looks like on a date? I once had a man with catastrophic thoughts tell me that he took a woman out for a first date to a Thai restaurant. Upon realizing that she did not like Thai food halfway through their meal, he thought, *She doesn't like Thai food? I love Thai food. This is never going to work out between the two of us. I am going to die single.*

Whoa, whoa, whoa. Let's not get ahead of ourselves here. But that is just what catastrophizing is all about. It is hard to see the possibilities of a relationship when you are so focused on how things will go terribly wrong.

Discounting the Positives

Collectively, as a society, we have been conditioned to respond to compliments negatively. I know I am guilty of quickly taking a compliment and shifting the focus to one of my flaws. Learning to simply say "thank you" took a lot of practice. Over time we have somehow learned from each other that it is not okay to appreciate the good things that people might say to us. Those who routinely discount the positives take this concept beyond accepting compliments. They are able to magically change any neutral or even positive situation into a negative one.

Some discounters have a big old BUT. They are practically "But"-heads. Anything that looks like it may be positive is quickly explained away with a "but." *Yeah, I'm a nice person … but that doesn't make me special. Sure, I volunteer a few times a week … but most of the time I am really selfish. Yeah, this dress is nice ... but I need to lose some weight.* Others simply disregard the positives by believing they do not count.

Those who regularly undermine themselves in this way have fallen into the habitual pattern of minimizing anything that is contrary to the dismal view they have of themselves. This distortion is like the Robin Hood of hot thoughts. It steals from the rich and gives to the poor. Or in this case, it steals from the positive and gives to the negative. It robs the discounter of all joy and makes life bleak. It contributes to low self-esteem, anxiety, depression, and feelings of inadequacy. Just what you need to set you up to be successful at dating, right? Of course not. It can cause unhealthy and unrealistic thoughts like, *He may have told me I looked beautiful tonight, but he didn't pull the chair out for me ... and that shows he isn't into me.* Or, *It doesn't count that he asked me out on a second date because he doesn't know the real me yet, and no one could ever love the real me.* Discounting the positive leads to an unrewarding experience in any endeavor, especially dating.

Overgeneralization

When you overgeneralize, you see one negative event as a pattern of failure or defeat that will never end. Instead of being open to other possibilities—or more than one answer—you take other times, experiences, or people and relate them back to that single negative experience or encounter.

When you are dating, it is likely that you will encounter an unpleasant experience or two. You might even have a downright awful time. It makes sense that those situations might stick with you a bit. However, that one situation is not an indication of how all subsequent dates will go. That is, unless you find yourself falling into the pattern of overgeneralizing. Then of course every subsequent date will be awful because you have foreseen it and are expecting it. Or even worse, you won't even get the chance to see how future dates will go because you have determined they will go badly and give up on the process. Pay attention to this warped way of thinking. Key words such as "always," "never," and "all" are cues that your thoughts might be distorted. An example of an overgeneralization is this: After going on a date with a serious bottom dweller you think, *What is the point of dating? I only meet jerks!* A thought like this can bring your personal life to a halt and prevent you from finding the relationship you deserve.

Emotional Reasoning

Feelings can be really strong. Sometimes too strong! And then there are some people who feel their emotions more deeply than others, making them quite overwhelming. However, even those of us who experience emotions within a normal range can find ourselves getting caught up in them. When we get all up in our feelings, we can lose our ability to think critically and use reason or logic. A recent encounter with a family member who had been feeling left out comes to mind. Because he was overwhelmed with general feelings of rejection, he concluded that I purposefully did not invite him to someone else's event and could not be convinced otherwise. Unwilling to look at the illogical premise of his thought that I would somehow be in charge of who could attend someone else's event, he dug into the idea. Disregarding the fact that I had never left him out of any event that I had ever thrown, I was unable to reason with him. Discounting the fact that he was actually told of the event by the person who was having it and reminded about it the night before, he couldn't think objectively and critically about the situation.

Emotional reasoning is what you do when you make assumptions based on how you feel. Your interpretation of what is real is based on your emotional state. Basically, because you feel it, it must be true. Just like thoughts are not fact, feelings are not fact either. Just because you intensely feel an emotion, that is not proof that your conclusions are valid. Dating evokes a whole bunch of emotions. Heck, you start feeling stuff before the actual date has happened. If you are prone to emotional reasoning you will likely find yourself believing the negative emotions you are feeling are based in reality. For example, you feel insecure and unattractive so you conclude that your date is going to think you are a dog! Nothing good can come from blindly following your negative emotions. Curiosity about your feelings—and remaining open to the possibility that your mind may have been taken hostage—can go a long way.

Personalizing

There are a lot of folks out there who just do not like dating. They believe that dating will uncover their defects and weaknesses. Walking into a situation where you believe you will be exposed as flawed or damaged is something that many of us would like to avoid. When a person holds a belief like this one, it is very easy to find evidence to support it—especially when you are feeling vulnerable and judged. So when things do not go the way you want them to, you believe the outcome of the date is attributed to your traits and qualities. The failure becomes yours and yours alone. You take "taking it personally" to a whole new level.

Personalizing is the mental process of assuming that what happens in your life and how other people behave are directly related to you. Of course, you do this without examining other credible explanations. Often, those who fall into this distorted thought pattern believe that they are inadequate and unworthy of love. Makes sense, right? If you think you are unlovable, it becomes very easy to blame yourself when dating is not successful. For example, *He dumped me because I was not a good girlfriend.* You forget to consider the fact that he has had three other "girlfriends" in the past six months.

What If-Ing

Ah, catastrophizing's first cousin, what if-ing. Remember Charlotte? She is a great champion at what if-ing. "What if eating that extra bite of bread messes up my chances of being cast at my audition?" "What if I am not a success and my mother is disappointed in me?" "What if therapy never works and I have wasted my time and money?" Each one of these "what ifs" seemed very plausible and had an immediate impact on her mood and her ability to engage in what was happening in the here and now. Her preoccupation with her weight made it difficult for her to perform at her audition. Her concern about not being successful made her less motivated to put in the work necessary to be a success. And her worry about therapy not working made her less engaged in the process while she was in my office. What if-ing can be an F-ing pain in the ass!

What if-ing is the warped pattern of asking yourself questions like, "What if (fill in the negative blank)?" You are preoccupied with what will happen if something goes wrong or if someone behaves badly. Instead of living in the moment, you find yourself worried about the future outcome. It is different than catastrophizing because catastrophic thoughts are predictions that you believe will come true. What if-ing is more about constantly pondering the possible negative outcomes of a situation. This type of anxious thinking is a great way to sabotage a good experience, because you are focused on an imaginable future occurrence and are not paying attention to what is really happening. Here's an example: *What if this first date turns into a second date, and then when we are dating, I fall in love with him and he cheats on me?* Hey there, what if you just get to know the guy right now and see if you are a good fit instead?

Labeling and Judging

As the human mind has developed over millennia we have really honed our ability to label and judge our environment. It is a useful skill that can help us to understand what is happening and how we want to engage with what is happening. Labeling is not always a cause for concern, but when we start to label people and focus on that label we tend to see them only as their label and not as the whole complex being that they are. Gigi had a knack for not only labeling the guys that she dated, but also for labeling herself. She labeled the guys she dated in the past as being "losers, jerks, opportunists, players, or guys who are only interested in getting laid and not on developing a meaningful relationship." That label became so fixed that it became a judgment of all men who showed an interest in her. To complicate things further, she labeled herself as un-datable and undesirable—because she does not believe she can attract a man of quality. As a result she felt hopeless, unlovable, and defective, and she gave up on the process.

Labeling and judging is a distorted way of thinking where you brand yourself or others with fixed critical and negative traits. It is thought that people who tend to label and judge people experience more stress than others who do not do the same. That is because a belief that people are their labels and cannot change leads to a strong reaction to the negative behaviors that you believe support your judgment. When you label someone, there is an assumption that this is who they are at their core— not just in the moment. Those who believe people can change are able to see a negative behavior as something that happened in the moment that may or may not be indicative of the kind of person they are. This flexibility in their thinking makes for a more enjoyable and open dating experience. It's impossible to be Zen and pleasant while dating if you have judgmental thoughts floating through your mind such as, *Look at the girl flirting with those guys over there—what a slut!* Or, *No one is talking to me—I'm undesirable.*

Once you become more acquainted with your thoughts, you will start to see how often you are falling into the trap of being led by your distorted thinking. Now that you are familiar with the kinds of warped thinking patterns you are drawn to, take some time to pay attention to when these hot thoughts surface. When they do, simply make note of them for now, and try to do so with curiosity instead of blaming or judgment. You are not your thoughts, and thoughts alone are not inherently good or bad. It is what we do with those thoughts that matter, and once you have learned to identify your distorted thinking you are well on your way to making some positive changes in your dating life. What do you think?

7 FEELING FREELY

Feeling freely is about getting all up in your feelings (any feelings) in a healthy way. Our human instinct is to protect and defend ourselves from anything that is harmful. When we view what we are feeling as being potentially harmful, we often find ourselves at war with ourselves. This happens particularly when we feel vulnerable, insecure, doubtful, discomfort, in pain, or anxious. We tend to react to these and other "harmful" feelings by retreating, negotiating them, fighting them, or surrendering. Retreating— or avoiding our feelings through escape, denial, or pushing them to the side—only delays the process of dealing with your feelings and prolongs the discomfort. Negotiating—or talking yourself out of your feelings—can leave you feeling frustrated, hopeless, uncared for, and invalidated. Fighting your feelings creates tension, fosters self-criticism, and only complicates the distressing emotions more. Surrendering to your feelings and allowing them to drive your behavior leaves you feeling out of control and powerless; this in turn can make your feelings seem stronger and more influential, merely because you no longer are confident that you can do anything differently when you are caught up in your feelings. None of these options are particularly effective, and you end up dealing (or not dealing) with your feelings in an unhealthy and unproductive way. Basically it is a big old waste of time and energy.

The reality is that there is no need to view our feelings as the enemy. We do not have to be at war with ourselves. It is possible to learn how to engage with our emotional and physical feelings with curiosity, openness, and acceptance—even when they are painful or upsetting.

EMOTIONAL FEELINGS

Emotional feelings are a way of describing the internal state of what is happening in our bodies and minds, usually related to our mood. They are representative of a moment in time. Feelings are not your house. You do not have to live in them. But that is not how we usually relate to them. In fact, it is pretty common for people to have an emotion and then label themselves with that emotion. For example, remember Ciara who had trouble "looking inside the box"? At times she struggles with feelings of insecurity. These feelings are especially activated when she is dating. If a relationship does not develop the way she wants it to, she often labels herself as an "insecure and unlovable person" and finds herself stuck in that feeling of insecurity for days or even weeks at a time. Is Ciara insecure and unlovable? No, of course not. In that moment she felt insecure because of the experience she was having, and she got stuck in her feelings. She surrendered and did not take time to look at the entire picture. She did not see how many people she has in her life who care about her. She did not place importance on how confident she is in her career. She mentally filtered out the positives in her life because she believed she *was* her feelings. Her habitual reaction to this feeling prevented her from seeing it as being momentary and letting it pass naturally.

We have a tendency to label our emotions in categories of good and bad or positive and negative. Some typical feelings labeled as "good," for example, are happy, joyful, confident, peaceful, and loving. Whereas angry, ashamed, jealous, fearful, and sad tend to be labeled as "bad" feelings. I have had

"Our human instinct is to protect and defend ourselves from anything that is harmful."

this conversation with many clients, friends, and family members over the years. People seem to have a pretty strong attachment to the labeling of these different feelings. "Of course, being angry is bad," is an argument I often hear. When I ask why it is bad, the answer usually goes something like, "Well, being angry doesn't change anything," "Being angry is a waste of time," or "Being angry is a sin." When I explain to them that anger is a natural, healthy reaction to triggering situations, they look at me like I have another head growing out of my neck. But it is true. There is nothing inherently wrong with being angry. It is an emotion just like any other emotion, and it is just as valid as any other emotion. It is human to feel angry from time to time. In fact, anger can be very useful. It can signal to you that there is something wrong, or that you are being treated unfairly. It can motivate you to remove yourself from an unhealthy environment or to advocate for yourself. Anger needs a new PR person because it has gotten a bad rap, like several other emotions that have been mislabeled. Anger is not the problem. Blindly being led by your anger and or letting your anger get out of control is the issue that needs to be addressed. When anger turns into rage and you are acting out on autopilot, then you are in real trouble. Otherwise, anger on its own is a necessary feeling that rounds out the human experience.

So if there is no such thing as a good or bad emotion, why do we categorize them in such a way? I think what we have here is a case of collective dichotomous mislabeling. We are thinking about feelings as being one or the other. But haven't there been times when feeling angry has also been kind of nice? Elizabeth, a former client, began treatment again after learning her husband was cheating on her and no longer wanted to be in their marriage. There was no warning ahead of time, and she spent the first couple of months feeling sad, confused, and worried about the future. When he finally moved out and collected his leftover items, she was overcome with feelings of anger. She felt angry that he had not been honest about his feelings sooner, that he had been manipulating her, that he was so irresponsible with her feelings, and that the life he promised her was taken away. Aware of her feelings, she simply witnessed them and was surprised by how nice it felt to finally feel angry. This is not always the way anger is experienced, but this example sheds light on the fact that anger does not have to be permanently categorized as "bad."

What we are really referring to when we talk about feelings is our personal description of a particular flavor of an experience. That flavor can range from being something we really enjoy to being something we really do not like—and anywhere in between. When I was a kid, the flavor and texture of raw tomatoes was not something I liked at all. Today, I am a tomato-eating fool! Or think about ice cream. Can we label all ice cream as being good or bad? Not really, right? There are way too many flavors to place a general label on all of the ice cream out there. I generally like ice cream, but if rum raisin is the only option I will probably pass. Similarly, the flavor of emotions can shift depending on a situation. That is why instead of looking at these feelings as being good or bad, or positive or negative, it is much more useful and accurate to think about them as being pleasant, unpleasant, or neutral.

Whether our feelings are pleasant, unpleasant, or neutral, they are always important to recognize and can always be useful. They are a signal to us of our internal reaction to something. They can help bring about awareness or recognition of our thoughts or behaviors. They can inform us that we are in need of care and consideration. However, most of us do not want to feel unpleasant feelings, so we avoid them. We do this with distraction, escaping, denial, ignoring, pushing them away, or talking ourselves out of them. Whatever strategy we employ usually prolongs the discomfort, and in many cases strengthens the intensity of the very feeling we are trying to avoid. Not to get all Yoda on you, but avoidance leads to suffering, and suffering leads to pain. It keeps us from embracing every part of ourselves and our experience. In essence, it stops us from living life fully.

Instead of backing away from the unpleasant feelings, there is a lot to be gained from being curious and tuning into them. It is in those teachable moments that we can learn what the

"Whether our feelings are pleasant, unpleasant, or neutral, they are always important to recognize and can always be useful."

source of our pain is, how to care for ourselves and how we can respond in a healthy way. When we do this, we transform our pain from a perceived weakness to a powerful strength. A strength that will give you confidence in even the most unpleasant situations. Instead of removing yourself from all dating sites (avoiding) because you have had a string of bad dates, you can take a break to investigate how you are feeling and what you need to do to soothe and care for yourself. You can then reapproach dating from this place of awareness, possibly setting clearer boundaries, reorganizing your list of priorities, and feeling confident that you can handle unpleasant feelings.

Another reason people back away from unpleasant feelings is that we tend to identify ourselves with our feelings. If we feel jealous of another and it is a familiar feeling, we might start to think that we *are* jealous. Even though it is one feeling among many that we experience during a single day, that one feeling becomes representative of who we are as a person. So we deny it—or ignore it—because we cannot stand to think of ourselves in that way. But this does not make the feeling go away. The only way to get past a feeling is to go through it. Not around it. Not under it. We have to go through it. It is our ability to recognize a feeling that allows us to break away from it and notice it simply as an experience—and not a representation of who you are. This clears the way for you to choose your response to what is happening, instead of reacting based on past experiences. This openness gives you a chance to act in manner that is suited for the situation—and in a way that you feel good about.

Feeling freely is not just about being open to unpleasant feelings. It is about being aware of *all* feelings. Sometimes it is not the unpleasant feelings that get us into trouble at all. The pleasant ones or neutral ones can also be problematic. For example, if you are prone to fall into one of the dating devices like "I need a hero," "Being overly partner-centered," or "loving love," it is your feelings of lust, impulsivity security, passion, admiration, comfort, and support that are front and center. All of those feelings can be quite nice. In fact, people tend to seek them out. They are often categorized as pleasant, and because of that they are not thought to be harmful in any way. But you know better by now. On their own, these feelings are just feelings. They are not problematic in any way. It is when you are not aware of what is triggering these feelings that a problem can arise.

Remember Hailey? She was in search of comfort and security in a relationship. She wanted a man to rescue her from her current lonely and poverty-stricken circumstances. The person she ended up with gave her what she was looking for, and she had very strong and pleasant feelings for him. They were the same strong and pleasant feelings she has had for almost all of her relationships when they are starting out. However, over time these relationships ended up turning from good to bad because she was not aware of her compulsive need to be in a relationship to feel complete and taken care of. She was not tuned into her need to have someone else be in control of her life and her dependence on others. She had no clue about this pattern in her life and how she was contributing to the cycle. With more mindful presence, Hailey could start to understand how her initial pleasant feelings were a signal that her neediness was being activated. This awareness may allow her to make better choices for herself instead of blindly following her impulses.

In between the pleasant and unpleasant, we have neutral feelings. It is just as important for you to be aware of when your emotional response to a situation is neither positive nor negative. Some might interpret neutral to mean feeling numb, "meh," or indifferent. This is not what I am talking about here. Neutral does not mean that you do not feel anything. Instead, it means that you are not triggered by an issue or situation. When you move from being triggered to no longer experiencing the moment as positive or negative, it then releases you to see things more realistically and respond more appropriately. In essence, neutral is what we strive for. It is a balanced state of being that brings about the clarity we need to act in our best interest.

"Neutral is what we strive for."

Neutral feelings don't sound very sexy though, right? When you meet someone, there is an expectation that you will have strong feelings in one direction or another. That you will get some sign that this person is either right or wrong for you—and we all often rely on our feelings as that sign. However, those polarized feelings can often be misleading or fleeting. They can also drive you to automatically react in one kind of patterned way. Neutral feelings have less of a hold on you, and that makes it possible for you to see the person you are with as a whole person instead of as a trigger for positive or negative feelings. This is a desired state of being that, with much practice, can be summoned at your will. But let's not get ahead of ourselves! We can start with some simple exercises to help you identify what kind of feelings you are having.

PHYSICAL FEELINGS

Your body is continuously experiencing sensations that often go unnoticed. Your heartbeat, for example, is always going—and if you take time to seek it out, you can feel the steady rhythm of life inside of you. If you are alive, then there is an energy flowing and pulsing through you constantly. It is quite beautiful and amazing when you stop to think about all that is happening within us that makes us functional. But just like with emotional feelings, we have unpleasant, pleasant, and neutral physical feelings. We have the same tendencies toward our physical feelings as we do toward our emotional feelings. When something feels unpleasant we do what we can to change it or ignore it. How many people do you know that have ailments but never seek any medical help for them or wait until a problem has become unbearable? We live in a society where medicating ourselves is normal. Every other commercial we see on television is about some drug that a pharmaceutical company is trying to push on us. Over-the-counter pain medications are readily available to numb our discomfort. I am not here to say that these forms of pain management are good or bad. I am simply saying that there is less emphasis on understanding the root cause of the problem and more of a focus on immediately annihilating what is unwanted.

Learning to be more connected to what is happening in our physical bodies can help us to be more connected with what is happening with us emotionally. It can also help us tune into what is happening in our minds.

Life is a sensory experience. However, we live much of the day out of touch with what our senses are taking in. How often do we take time to experience a beautiful sunrise or sunset, enjoy the feeling of brushing our hair, or paying attention to how our body reacts to a delicious meal? No, instead of doing this we are usually two steps ahead of ourselves, planning out our days or vegging out on television, or sucked into our smartphones as life passes us by. Bringing mindfulness to the body means getting familiar with your five senses again. Let me reintroduce you to the Five Senses: seeing, hearing, smelling, tasting, and touching.

By getting in touch with our five senses, we are accessing a way of taking in information different from our usual one. In Western society we often rely on our minds as the primary informant. But as we have talked about before, the mind can be tricky and deceptive. Your senses are more straightforward and are an equally good source of information about your current experience. It is useful to practice taking in and getting reacquainted with all sensations, including the unpleasant ones that we actively avoid. Resisting your unpleasant physical feelings and sensations takes a whole lot of energy and is not an effective use of time. In terms of dating, it does not help you to waste energy or avoid relevant sensory information that can help you to understand what is happening in the moment. By learning to take in all sensations, you become aware of the total experience—not just what feels good to you. For example, you may be out with a charming, good-looking suitor who has so much swag, and everything he says and does makes your feel excited, sexy, and desirable. However, you ignore that pit in your stomach that could be informing you that there is something that you don't trust about this guy. Every time he tells an elaborate story about how successful he is and the circle he runs with, that sensation in your stomach reappears ... but you feel so turned on by him that you not even aware of it. Then when the bill comes and five of his credit cards are rejected, you are left with an $800 dinner bill because he ordered four courses in a five-star restaurant and just had to get this amazing bottle of wine he had on vacation in Ibiza with Leo DiCaprio last month.

Mindfulness of the body takes time and practice. We often relate to our bodies in a negative way. We focus more on its flaws than on how amazing our bodies are and all that they do for us. The body is often referred to as a vessel for your soul or your spirit. If we relate to it in this way, then we can appreciate it as sacred and something to be cared for and proud of. Instead of focusing on our outward appearance, we can appreciate it and invest in the maintenance of it. We can learn to get back into our body and get in tune with all of its sensations. We can practice noticing an itch and just letting it be without reactively scratching it. We can enrich our sensual experiences with intimate partners by really feeling their touch—instead of being in our minds and focusing on how we look or whether or not we are satisfying them. You can live life fully, experiencing everything, instead of letting life pass you by.

"In terms of dating, it does not help you to waste energy or avoid relevant sensory information that can help you to understand what is happening in the moment."

Physical pain is a real issue. Figuring out a way to manage pain and discomfort can be time-consuming and mentally taxing. Anger, frustration, sadness, hopelessness, and fear can overwhelm you. Medication can help with the pain, but it does not take care of the emotions and can often cause additional emotional strain because of side effects. Resistance to pain can intensify it by creating more stress. We know that stress is linked to many painful physical conditions. With mindfulness, you can learn how to live with the pain in a way that improves your day-to-day experience. Meditation in particular has been proven to be effective in significantly decreasing pain. By learning to sit with pain, accept it, and not resist it, you can have increased mental stability and be more at ease.

When I began my journey with becoming more aware of my feelings, I found that one of the most effective ways to get in touch with them was to practice mindfulness meditation. As human beings we have feelings all the time. When I meditate, my feelings are the first thing I sense. Others might be more aware of thoughts when they meditate, but for me it is what I am feeling and sensing that I recognize clearly. But even if you are more aware of your thoughts than your sensations, you are sure to experience a few different feelings during a sitting. Because of this, mindfulness meditation is the ideal circumstance to practice becoming aware of and responding to those feelings. Your breath is your anchor. When your attention is drawn away from your breath due to a feeling, don't force yourself to refocus on your breath immediately. Spend some time keeping your awareness there with your feelings and resting in that sensation, whether pleasant, unpleasant, or neutral.

When you are on a date and you feel emotionally triggered, it may not always be convenient to take a meditation break. (Not to say that sometimes a trip to the bathroom for a pause may not be in order.) My hope is that you will begin to practice mindfulness meditation regularly so that a formal meditation break won't be necessary for you to respond to your feelings. A daily practice is recommended to build tolerance, skills, and confidence in your ability. By doing this you will strengthen your mindfulness muscles, which will allow you to effectively practice mindfulness anytime and anywhere. This is one of the great things about mindfulness. It is always there with you as a tool to be called upon. So how do you do it? There are many ways to go about it. Here are some practices I like.

Five-Step Mindfulness of the Body

1. **Name it**. This is not like a stray animal that you will not have the heart to give away if you name it. This is different. Giving your emotions a name is a way to acknowledge that a feeling is present, and it is an important part of the process of letting it go. If you realize you are testy, you can say to yourself, "I am

feeling irritable." Notice, I did not say, "I am irritable." By saying you are your feelings, you equate yourself as being that feeling instead of it being a description of what you are experiencing in the moment. It is important to make that distinction. Words matter!

2. **Accept it**. You do not have to protect yourself from awkward or difficult emotions. In fact, doing so only complicates them. Instead, you can learn to receive or embrace the feeling. This is an act of self-care and is the opposite of what we often do instead. We typically criticize and punish ourselves for having "bad" feelings. This lack of self-compassion is a reaction to our suffering and has negative consequences. When we are open to what is happening in the moment, we make room for the discovery that we are not our emotions. No, we are much more than that. Acceptance and patience allows us to witness our feelings without becoming them. It creates a spaciousness around our emotions that makes room for a healthy response.

3. **Recognize it**. The first thing to acknowledge is that feelings are not permanent. They are an expression of what is happening right now. But just as this moment will pass, so will your emotions. They are ever-moving, here one moment and gone another—like yellow cabs taxiing around on any given NYC day. This does not mean that you should dismiss your emotions. That is why the next thing to acknowledge is the cause of your distress. Where did this feeling come from? Why is it present now? There can be many reasons why you are experiencing a particular emotion. Something could have occurred that you had a strong emotional response to. You know by now that thoughts can impact how you feel. Was there an idea or worry that was the cause? Maybe it is more than just a thought— maybe it is an actual belief or value that you hold that

created the feeling. Perhaps your feelings are justified, and perhaps they are an automatic or habitual response to a similar experience in the past. Recognizing the cause can help you discern that.

1. **Respond to it:** Every step before this one has paved the way for you to choose what you want to do next. You have all the information you need to decide how to respond to your emotions. That may take the form of not responding at all. The previous steps may lead you to not needing to do anything more than having mindful presence and bringing your feelings into your awareness. Or perhaps reflecting on your emotions has given you some insight into what you need to do next. Wherever this process leads you, it is important for you listen to your gut and stay present. The trick here is to not get ahead of yourself and worry about what will happen if you trust in yourself. Instead try to remain open to what is and what will be.

Mindfulness of the Senses

1. Take a seat. I like to practice this seated because sitting is a great way to be fully aware of your body.

2. Take a moment to anchor yourself in your breath. Feel the sensation of the air going into your nose, the natural pause that occurs after, the exhalation through your mouth and the natural pause after. Do this until you feel grounded, maybe 5–10 times.

3. Remind yourself of what the five senses are. Seeing, hearing, tasting, smelling, and touching.

4. Ask yourself, "What am I seeing?" For example, white walls, the Empire State Building, the Meatpacking

District, large flat-screen TV, my husband playing with his iPhone on our bed, clothes on the floor.

5. Ask yourself, "What am I hearing?" For example, the sound of construction in always-changing Manhattan, horns from the cars below, my breathing, the vague sound of conversation from outside of our room.

6. Ask yourself, "What am I tasting?" For example, coffee I am drinking, the milk in the coffee. (I'm really drinking coffee right now as I am writing this!)

7. Ask yourself, "What am I smelling?" For example, the patchouli lavender vanilla lotion on my skin, the coffee next to me, Miss Jessie's Jelly Soft Curls in my hair.

8. Ask yourself, "What am I touching or feeling physically?" I feel my feet on the carpeted floor, my legs against the workbench, the hair framing my face, the coolness of the room temperature, and a rumble in my tummy.

Body Scan

This popular mindfulness meditation practice can be helpful for those who are experiencing physical pain, as well as those who just want to get more in touch with what is happening in their bodies. Make sure to practice this at a time when you are wide awake. It can be deeply relaxing, and you might find yourself napping before you know it otherwise.

The purpose of the body scan is to bring awareness to different parts of your body, notice what is happening there, and do nothing but sit with the sensation. The reactive part of ourselves wants to change a feeling that might be unpleasant or uncomfortable. The body scan teaches you to be more focused, to let go of the need to be doing something, and to listen to your body.

Remember, your mind will wander. When this happens, notice

what you are thinking, be curious about where it came from, and refocus yourself on your breath and the body part you are tuned into. Don't get too serious about it. This exercise can be challenging, but it can be done in a lighthearted way that can help to take the pressure off of you to do it right. Just try your best.

1. Start by lying down on a mat on the floor, or on your bed. Try to find a location with minimal distractions that is warm and cozy. Make yourself comfortable and gently close your eyes.

2. Take a moment to anchor yourself in your breath. Feel the sensation of the breath going in and out. Notice the rise and fall of your abdomen. Bring attention to the steady rhythms of your breath.

3. Next bring awareness to where your body is making contact with the floor, mat, or bed. What parts of your body are touching the surface you are lying on? What does that feel like? As you continue to breathe, let yourself become more connected with the surface you are on.

4. Remember, the intention of this exercise is to simply get in touch with what is happening in your body. Not to change it or fix it. Only to be with whatever sensations are present.

5. Now, focus your attention on your feet. Begin with your left toes. Notice any sensations, pulses, itches, warmth, touching, pain, or energies flowing through that part of your body as you continue to breathe in and out.

6. Using your breath as a tool to connect with that body part, imagine breathing in through your nose, into your lungs, through your abdomen, past your pelvis, down your legs, and out through your toes. Then

breathe out, and imagine the breath passing back through your toes and back up through your body and out of your mouth. Continue doing this a few times.

7. Next, gently move your focus from your toes to your entire left foot. Pay attention to the tops of your foot, the heel, the sole, the instep, the ankles, the skin, bones, and joints. Are you making contact with the surface you are lying on with any part of your foot? What sensations are present? Breathe through your foot the same way you did through your toes a few times.

8. Now, release your attention from your foot and focus it on your left leg starting at your calf. Repeat the process of noticing any contact with the surface, paying attention to any sensation and then breathing in and out of it. Then move on to the left shin, the knee, and the thigh.

9. With the same openness and curiosity, move to your right toes, foot, ankle, and so on. Once you have finished with your right thigh, you can move your awareness to the sensation in the rest of your body, starting with the pelvis and moving on to the abdomen, chest, back, left shoulder, left arm, left elbow, left hand, left fingers, right fingers, right hand, right elbow, right arm, right shoulder, neck, head, and face.

10. Breathe in and out while sensing each body part in the same way you did when you started with your toes, as if you are breathing through that part. Let go of each part with the same intention of releasing that body part and bringing your attention to a new body part. If unpleasant sensations arise, pay attention to them, breathe into them, and do your best to release them in the same way.

11. When you have finished scanning each body part take a moment to bring awareness to the body as a whole. Let your breathing flow in and out of you with the intention of feeling freely. And do not forget to honor your practice and your efforts at the end.

This is it! This is the start of you taking back your power by not giving in to your emotional or physical feelings and allowing them to control you. Be honest with yourself about how your feelings have been driving you. It is time for you to confront your fears about dating and to become more acquainted with your unpleasant, pleasant, and neutral feelings. That familiarity with your reactions and automatic thoughts is just what you need to help you stop avoiding yourself—and start accepting all parts of who you are and what you experience. Not until you are open to your feelings will you ever get the chance to live life fully and be your true self. That is true whether you are dating someone or not. Self-acceptance can give you the confidence to date—being open, genuine, and in control of yourself and your choices, no matter what feelings you are having.

PART THREE
PREPARING FOR MINDFUL DATING

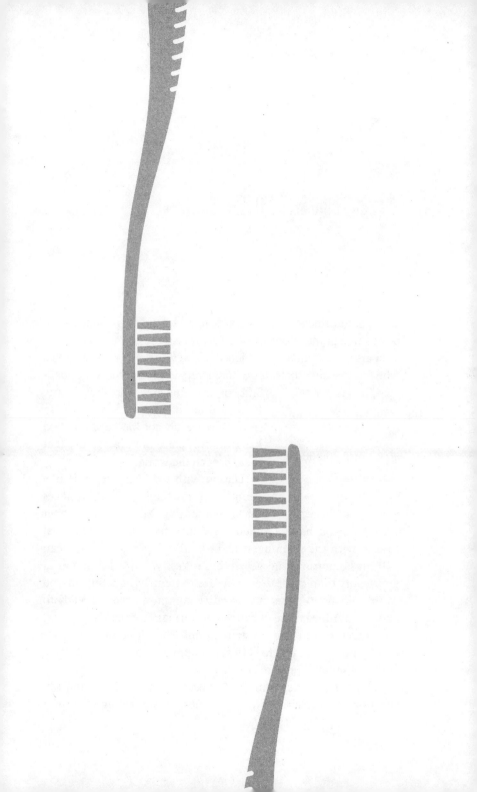

8 BUILDING SELF-ESTEEM

Being comfortable in your own skin is a quality that eludes all of us at some point in our lives. Self-criticism, rejection, and doubt are part of the human experience. However, there are some of us who feel insecure like it is our job! Every experience has the possibility of revealing how worthless we are. Being around others serves as a way to show how we do not measure up. And it is from this place of vulnerability that we approach the world.

> "Self-esteem is a confidence and satisfaction in yourself and your abilities."

Dating with low self-esteem is like going to bat for the New York Yankees with a big old secret you have been hiding. Yes, you are a super star! Yes, you have a ridiculously lucrative, decade-long deal to play with the winningest team in all of sports. Yes, you can still hit home runs and get on base. Yes, you are still better at your sport than most. Yes, you are extremely hot! But all you can think about is that investigative committee who is ready to expose your illegal use of banned performance-enhancing drugs, and therefore you end up striking out when it counts. As your batting average begins to suffer, so does your confidence. Dating with low self-esteem leads to striking out.

So what is self-esteem? Self-esteem is a confidence and satisfaction in yourself and your abilities. It is a feeling of respect for yourself and an honoring of who you are and what you can contribute as an individual. This pride and positive (or neutral) self-regard is based on how you relate to yourself. It is not based on what others think about you, and it is not reflective of who you are fundamentally. This is where we can get really messed up. We get so caught up in proving our self-worth to others that we become dependent on their approval to make us feel good about ourselves. But even with that approval, if we do not have good self-esteem, we will find the proof we need to support the underlying negative beliefs we have about our worth. We take this to mean that I really am worthless, not good enough, or unlovable— when all it really means is that *I think* I am worthless, not good enough, or unlovable. You see what I did there? By putting the words "I think" in front of the statement, I am able to differentiate between a fact and an idea. Because that is just what this is. It is simply an idea. You are feeling insecure not because you are not good enough, but because you *think* you are not good enough. You see, self-esteem is all about your internal experience and not about what has happened externally or how other people see you.

Scott had a history of dating women whom he was initially very attracted to and then at some point in the relationship he began to feel angry at them. From his point of view, he had given each one of the women he had dated the world, and they all took advantage of him. He was raised to be a gentleman by his mother who was an alcoholic and dependent on him to care for her. He believed he knew how to take care of a woman, but he never felt his needs were met or even considered.

Early in treatment, we were able to identify that Scott had trouble expressing his needs to the women he dated. He also did not set boundaries or limits with these women, and he often put his needs to the side so he could make them happy. If they were happy with him he felt good about himself in the moment. But that feeling did not last for long, and over time he began to resent them for always taking and never giving. He thought

Exercise: Place the words "I think" in front of a belief or thought you have to get some distance from it.

that if they really loved him then they would know to care for him. When that expectation was not met, his self-esteem suffered.

Scott, like many other people, was in the habit of looking for the approval of others to validate his own value. The repeated seeking of validation from others led to him becoming a people pleaser. When you are a people pleaser, what others want is more important than what you want because you want them to like you. If you do not cooperate with their requests you worry that they will reject you or be upset with you. As a result you lose touch with your own limits and boundaries and are at risk of being taken advantage of. Eventually, you can grow to feel resentful of others and angry at yourself because your needs are not being met. It is your responsibility to yourself to set limits. Even good people can find themselves taking advantage of a pushover because that is the dynamic that is created. By setting boundaries, you take care of yourself. You also protect yourself from being used and free yourself from the burden of blindly putting others first. This was a skill that Scott had never learned. He was conditioned at a young age to put the needs of others first. But with practice he was able to find his voice and began to see his needs as important too.

As we have discussed in previous chapters, our view of ourselves can be pretty narrow. Imagine looking at the night sky through a straw. Not a city sky, but a country or desert sky where the stars are visible. It is possible that you won't see even one star. Take away that straw and there might be hundreds of stars for you to gaze upon. Now get this: the spot of night sky you see through that straw is said to contain 10,000 galaxies! And we see nothing! We might conclude there are no stars in the sky. This is like how we see ourselves. Left to our own bias, we might conclude there is nobody out there who would be interested in us. We can become so fixated on one part of ourselves (that we view as negative) and in turn make our self-esteem plummet so low that we forget to look at the hundreds or even thousands of other examples and pieces of evidence that disprove that view.

Mindfulness can be helpful in building lasting self-esteem. With the awareness and self-acceptance that comes with a mindfulness practice, you can develop self-esteem that will stand up to the occasional comparison to what other people are doing or acquiring. You can become skilled at keeping your view of yourself intact in the face of disappointment or rejection. One way mindfulness helps you cultivate unwavering self-esteem is through the practice of being nonjudgmental about your thoughts and emotions. As you become less critical of what is happening in your mind and of what you are feeling, you will start to have less of a binary attitude and find that you take a more neutral position within yourself.

Mindfulness also teaches us to focus on the present moment. When we are feeling worthless and down on ourselves, we tend to think about other negative experiences that can make our self-esteem take a dive. By focusing on the here and now and all that is present in this moment, we can gently focus ourselves away from the habit of ruminating on old situations. We can see that this is how we feel right now, but we will not always feel that way. We can listen to ourselves and understand where these negative thoughts and feelings are coming from. We can figure out what we need in the moment and how we can care for ourselves in a healthy and productive way. We can allow the feelings to pass instead of forcing them to be the way we want them to be. We can do this with confidence, because we trust in our skills and ability to handle unpleasant feelings. This in turn will build our self-efficacy, which is the belief that we have the ability to get the results we want. And what do you think comes from that? More self-esteem, of course!

It can be difficult to break free from habitual negative thinking. The thoughts are so ingrained that you do not even have to summon them up. Your autopilot kicks in and is in control. And because they are so familiar and constant, you tend to just accept them or not even take notice of them as they shape how you are feeling and behaving. There is comfort and familiarity in these habitual thoughts. This is called a secondary gain, and it is a trick we play on ourselves to stay

> Self-efficacy is the belief that we have the ability to get the results we want.

stuck right where we are, instead of moving toward self-respect, hope, progress, and opportunity.

Hailey, who if you will remember was prone to suffering from the "I need a hero" dating device, had very little self-respect and virtually no confidence in her abilities to be happy on her own. She looked to others to provide her with a sense of self-worth, citing their interest in her as proof that she was a valuable person. When her relationships went sour, instead of dealing with her fears of loneliness and failure, she fell into the same pattern by seeking out another partner to rescue her from her life. And when that did not work out, she blamed herself for their bad behavior, which led to a depressed mood and more negative thinking.

Hailey was so focused on the secondary gains of seeking comfort and being rescued that she threw away any chance to feel self-sufficient, self-reliant, or empowered. She stuck with what she knew because she had no trust in her ability to handle unpleasant emotions or make changes in her life. She quickly moved from one relationship to another to avoid the discomfort that came along with looking too closely at her life.

Mindfulness helps you to slow down. By taking the time to be with what is happening in the moment, you give yourself an opportunity to see the entire picture. Even if some of it is unpleasant or upsetting, you are able to cope with the discomfort. By simply being with what is happening in the present moment, you stop yourself from focusing on what might happen in the future or what has happened in the past—and you turn off your autopilot. With your autopilot off, you slow things down. You have more awareness about what is going on and the opportunity to make a choice about how you want to move forward presents itself. With that choice comes a sense of control over your life that brings about more confidence in your ability to make good decisions for yourself. With more confidence comes a calmer state of being, one where you feel empowered. One where you feel secure. Security, empowerment, and confidence are building blocks of good self-esteem.

Hailey was pretty resistant to learning mindfulness. She did not believe she had the ability to sit with her emotions. The thought of allowing herself to feel unpleasant emotions was terrifying to her. She would often roll her eyes at me and tell me she did not believe in mindfulness. We spent a lot of time orienting her to the practice of mindfulness as a real and effective evidence-based treatment and not some mystic mumbo jumbo.

"Security, empowerment, and confidence are building blocks of good self-esteem."

Underneath all of her skepticism and resistance was the fear of trying something new and failing. She imagined herself being unable to handle her feelings and having a breakdown. So we made a deal. I promised to teach her some self-soothing skills, work on increasing her interpersonal skills, and help her to build a self-care practice. Once this basic foundation was established, we began slowly. We rated the thoughts that caused her the most anxiety and made her feel bad about herself, and we began to sit with the emotions that caused her the least distress. As she began to master the skill of sitting with her thoughts and emotions nonjudgmentally, she began to feel more confident in her ability to handle more challenging thoughts. And we were off! In time, Hailey was able to make choices about what she wanted to do and what was in her best interest. She made plenty of bad choices along the way, but she was better equipped to handle them, identify the problematic behaviors, and learn from them. She had more awareness about when her automatic pilot kicked in and what triggered it. She gained more respect for herself and felt a sense of pride in her ability to take care of herself without being dependent on others.

One common misconception about mindfulness is that it has the power to make your problems go away. As if it is a magic trick that will make your life stressors disappear. That is not the case. You can't snap your magic fingers and say, "Bippity boppity boo!" and get yourself out of your troubles. By practicing the skills of mindfulness, you become better able to approach your problems in a calm, effective way. Mindfulness helps you to see things as they are and make wiser choices for yourself, instead of just reacting to situations and regretting it later. As you build your mindfulness skills, you will automatically begin to feel better about yourself and more comfortable in your own skin because you will learn to trust yourself and honor your choices. Bippity boppity bam!

SELF-SOOTHING SKILLS

Self soothing is all about engaging in activities that help to calm and relax you in a gentle and kind way. It can come more naturally to some than others. Some people have an innate ability to nurture themselves in a soothing way or have had it modeled for them by a parent or other influential person in their lives. Other people have never known they could soothe themselves because they have never been exposed to how to do it. I encourage you to try all of these different techniques, find the ones that work best for you, and cultivate your practice. By cultivating or continuing to develop your practice through regular utilization of the skills, you will get the full benefits of the exercises. And when you need to call upon your self-soothing skills, you will be able to access them because they are a part of your regular routine.

Some people might find that they feel guilty or undeserving of this type of attention or relaxation. We will discuss this feeling of guilt more in the next chapter about self-compassion. However, you should know that those feelings and thoughts are normal, especially if this type of practice is new to you. It may take some time to get used to doing this for yourself. Try reminding yourself that you have a right to these natural pleasures, just like anyone else, and refocus yourself on the exercises.

"I'm Worth It" Meditation

The purpose of this exercise is to reinforce that you are worth the time, attention, and effort it takes to build your self-esteem. I suggest you use it before doing any of the exercises listed below in each of the categories for self-soothing, interpersonal skills, and self-care. This will help to connect the intellectual and emotional parts of yourself.

1. Start by finding a comfortable place to sit, stand, or lie down. It really does not matter what position you are in, as long as you can focus on the exercise.

2. Next, take three mindful breaths in through your nose and out of your mouth. Make sure to pay attention to the sensations of breath in your chest, abdomen, nose, mouth, and throat.

3. If you do not feel grounded quite yet, repeat the previous step until you are feeling present.

4. Now, state the mantra, "I am worth it" while taking another full cycle of breathing. Once that cycle is complete, take another full cycle of breathing.

5. Next, add on to the mantra and state, "I am worth the time" while taking another full cycle of breathing. Once that cycle is complete, take another full cycle of breathing.

6. Then state the mantra, "I am worth the attention" while taking another full cycle of breathing. Once that cycle is complete, take another full cycle of breathing.

7. Finally, state the mantra, "I am worth the effort" while taking another full cycle of breathing. Once that cycle is complete, take another full cycle of breathing. Take three final cycles of mindful breaths in through your nose and out through your mouth. When you have finished your final cycle, open your eyes when you are ready, and proceed to what is next.

Singular Sensory Self-Soothing

This exercise is similar to one we have discussed before, with a slight twist. It is practice in focusing in on *one* of your five senses and taking in all of the information that presents itself through that sense. As with all mindfulness exercises, you are practicing awareness while maintaining a nonjudgmental stance. Continue to use your breath as an anchor, as in other mindfulness exercises you have practiced. Once you have practiced using one sense, you may find that you have done enough—or that you want to continue on by engaging more of your senses. Do what feels right for you in the moment, but one sense is plenty.

- **Sight:** Feast your eyes on stunning sights. Take a stroll in a lovely neighborhood. Walk around the botanical gardens. Look at a beautiful picture. Get lost in a museum. Walk through a park. Watch a show or movie with beautiful scenery. Buy some pretty flowers to gaze upon in your home. Do so with the intention of taking in what you are seeing in detail, without judgment.
- **Sound:** Listen to soothing music. Play an instrument. Listen to a relaxing book on tape or radio program. Sit at a playground and listen to children playing. Listen to the ocean, waterfall, babbling brook, or other sound of nature—either in person or on a recording. Pay attention to all sounds that are present, and let different sounds come and go. For example, while sitting at the beach and listening to the ocean you might hear a flock of seagulls go by. Take that sound in, and once it has passed refocus yourself on another sound.
- **Taste:** Enjoy a nice cup of tea or coffee. Try your favorite treat. Pick a few things to taste, and enjoy the array of different flavors that are present. Take time to relish the taste, how it feels going down your throat and how your body reacts to it.
- **Smell:** Diffuse your favorite essential oils. Light a soothing candle. Boil three cups of water, two cinnamon sticks and ginger, and let your house soak up the aroma. Apply a nice-smelling lotion to your hands. Find a garden or park, and enjoy the different natu-

ral scents. Go to a bakery and take in the fresh and comforting smell. Take time to recognize all of the different smells that are present.

- **Touch:** Pet your animal. Brush your hair. Snuggle a baby. Put on your favorite comfy piece of clothing. Wrap yourself in a soft blanket. Take a bath or a dip in the pool or the ocean. Do the dishes. Wash your hands. Give yourself or someone else a massage. Play with silly putty. Feel the temperature, softness, wetness, texture, smoothness, roughness, dryness, mushiness, or any other way it feels at your fingertips.

Taking the time to engage just one of your senses is an investment in yourself. Allow yourself to be proud of yourself for making that investment. Let that sense of pride be with you as you go about your day.

Total Sensory Self-Soothing

Total sensory self-soothing exercises, like the one below, allow you to focus on the here and the now by helping you to get in touch with each one of your senses. By practicing being in the present moment and returning to that moment when your mind wanders, you are able to attend to your needs as they present themselves.

Mindful Cooking

Cooking is an activity that is a total sensory experience. You can engage all five senses at once while doing something that has a tangible positive outcome. You can connect with your food in a new way. Even those who believe they cannot cook have no excuse anymore with home delivery services like Blue Apron that give you recipes and portion out your food. All you have to do is follow the directions and you can cook a gourmet meal. You can also keep it simple with just a few colorful ingredients and still benefit from this exercise. For example, you can make a portobello mushroom and red pepper quesadilla, or a goat cheese and spinach scrambled egg—or even healthy, two-ingredient banana oatmeal cookies! The possibilities are endless. So start practicing your Gordon Ramsay or Julia Child impression and get cooking.

The idea is to cook while paying attention to each one of your senses, so eliminate distractions (phone, music, television, etc.) There is so much to take in while cooking. If a thought comes to mind, acknowledge it and refocus on what your senses are picking up. The exercise begins at the very first touch of an ingredient, the sizzling of butter in the pan or pouring of a liquid. What colors are you seeing? What sounds are you hearing? Any smells? What do the ingredients feel like in your hands?

With each additional ingredient, be sure to pay attention to the subtle changes in aroma, consistency of the food, temperature, and so on. Be aware of how your body is reacting to the food. Is your stomach growling? Is your mouth watering? As you cook, make sure you taste your food. Does it need more seasoning? What does it feel like in your mouth? Is there texture? Is the taste pleasing to you?

Check in with yourself. How are you feeling? Has your mood changed? Are you relaxed by the activity? Are you feeling anxious about what you have to do next, or are you confident about your skills? Don't try to change your feelings. Simply observe them and then refocus yourself on your sense.

This practice will strengthen your ability to gently guide yourself back to the task at hand. It will also help you to manage any unpleasant emotions that come up in a productive and soothing way. As you incorporate this exercise into your routine, you will become more confident in your cooking and mindfulness skills. In time, this exercise can become an enjoyable experience with a delicious outcome.

INTERPERSONAL SKILLS

Interpersonal skills help to build self-esteem by improving your ability to express and advocate for yourself in a way that is effective, which in turn improves relationships.

Delayed Response Exercise

If you are a people pleaser who finds yourself doing things that you do not actually want to do and then being upset about it later, you are stuck in the habit of saying yes without assessing what is in your best interest. By practicing a delayed response to a request, you will give yourself an opportunity to process your thoughts and feelings about doing what is asked of you. By bringing your thoughts and feelings into your awareness, you can assess why you are thinking and feeling what you are, and figure out what it is truly in your best interest to do. We call this behavior modification because you are changing your actions based on taking in all of the information, instead of acting on autopilot.

Setting boundaries and limits is a necessary part of building self-esteem. Think about it. How can you respect yourself if you allow others' needs to be prioritized over your own? Making your needs a priority is essential to feeling good about you. When you learn to do this you see what a relief it is to stop doing the things you don't want to do. Remember this: Saying no to others allows you to say yes to yourself. Here's how to start:

1. Recognize that something is being asked of you.

2. Take a brief moment to breathe in and out, grounding yourself in the present moment.

3. Tell the person who is making the request that you need to think about it.

4. Take time to assess what you are thinking.

5. Now ask yourself what you are feeling.

6. With curiosity and openness, investigate why you are thinking and feeling the way you are.

7. Decide what is in your best interest to do.

8. Respond to the person who made the request with your decision.

It may take you a few minutes to decide or a day or two. Take whatever time you need to get a full understanding of what you truly want to do. This is your right!

Effective Communication with the Feedback Wheel

It is difficult to feel good about yourself if you are not able to express what you think, feel, and need effectively. Without these skills you can find yourself withholding important information, not advocating for yourself, becoming a pushover, and/or feeling out of control. This can lead to resentment, anger, self-loathing, depression, acting out, and more.

I often use the feedback wheel with couples as a way for them to work through conflict or issues that arise, but it is also very useful tool in communicating with friends, family, acquaintances, coworkers, or anyone else. And the bonus is that you will be a pro at using this skill when you are in a relationship, improving the chances of successful communication with your partner!

The feedback wheel is a tool to be used with the person you are hoping to communicate with. Note I said "with"—not "to"—them. So it is important that you ask that person if it is a good time to talk about something that has been on your mind. If they say no, ask when would be a good time, and plan to talk then. If they say yes, then proceed. Make sure to have this conversation with pure intentions of simply communicating something important from a place of love. You can do this by opening with a what's called a gift statement such as, "You are my dearest friend and our relationship means so much to me," or, "I am so proud of all of the progress you have made in your career." Follow the next four steps:

1. State the facts and only the facts. That is, share what happened or what you saw in the most objective form. By doing so you minimize the chances that the person you are speaking to will feel attacked or become defensive.

2. Share what the situation made you believe. Make sure to use "I" statements. This puts the ownership on you for how you assigned meaning to a situation. You take responsibility for your role in the matter being discussed. It helps to keep the communication a collaborative one. For example: "I have been interpreting your recent late nights at work to mean that you do not want to spend time with me."

3. Explain how that thought or belief made you feel. For example: "I feel sad, rejected, and lonely." Remember to differentiate between thoughts and feelings here so the person you are speaking to does not feel blamed. You should have plenty of practice doing this by now.

4. Express what you would like to happen instead. This can be very challenging. Especially for those who are not used to expressing their needs. But that is why it is a valuable exercise. Instead of expecting the person to just know what they should do, you are being clear about what you want. This cuts down on future resentment toward the person you are talking to. It is always your responsibility to be clear about your needs and to take care of yourself in the process. That doesn't mean that you won't want the person who upset you to make you feel better. However, you can't expect them to make you feel better. That is not their responsibility. But you can collaboratively work toward resolution by sharing what you would like to happen in the future.

Once you have completed the four steps of the Feedback Wheel, do your best to let go of any outcome. There is value in doing this exercise no matter what the outcome. By learning to express yourself you will begin to feel more confident in your ability to advocate for yourself, and you will experience increased satisfaction in the way you are able to communicate with others effectively.

SELF-CARE

Self-care describes the actions you take to improve your overall mental and physical health. Some might view these actions as being self-indulgent, but studies prove over and over again that self-care is a necessary part of the healthy development of an individual. Those who engage in self-care have higher self-esteem and tend to have more empathy for others. So you are actually helping yourself and others by taking the time needed to care for yourself.

Mindful Mornings

Many of us start the day by hitting snooze over and over again and then rushing out of the door to get to wherever we have to be on time. By doing this, we sacrifice the opportunity to feel good about our appearance in order to get a few more minutes of beauty rest. Trust me, those 15–30 extra minutes of sleep are not doing the trick!

The goal here is to be the best version of yourself. You are creating a soothing routine for yourself that communicates that you are worth the effort and that starts you off on a positive note. This includes but is not centered on taking the time to look your best. Self-care means something different to us all. Below is a list of things you can do for yourself that will help you mindfully move through your morning. As with all mindfulness exercises, you are doing these things with a mindful presence. You are nonjudgmentally engaging in these activities, and when your mind wanders from the task at hand, you are acknowledging the thought, accepting it for what it is, and then intentionally refocusing yourself on what you are doing. Your breath serves as an anchor helping you to return to the here and now.

1. **Eat mindfully.** Set your intention to pay attention to eating. As you prepare to eat, examine your food. What do you see? Color? Shape? Pay attention to how your body reacts to it. How does your stomach feel?

Are you hungry? How does it smell? Is there texture? How does the food feel on your fork or spoon? Is it heavy or light? Put the food in your mouth. How does it feel? Is it smooth, hard, slippery, rough, or something else? How does it feel on your tongue, lips, and teeth? As you swallow, pay attention to the way it feels going down your throat. How do you feel once all the food is out of your mouth? Are you hungry, satisfied, full, or stuffed? Continue until your food is gone. Bonus: this is something you can practice on a date to bring yourself back into the moment with a simple glass of water.

2. **Journal.** Take a moment to ground yourself by going through a few cycles of breathing, and then write in a stream-of-consciousness style— let whatever is present come out. It does not have to be in any format or make sense to anybody else. This is an exercise in getting what is in your mind on to paper. Once you have finished, take a look at what you wrote. Do you connect with what was written? Does it seem as if someone else wrote it? Is there another way of looking at what you wrote? Remind yourself that what is written is simply an expression of what was happening in that moment and not necessarily representative of the truth.

3. **Set time to meditate.** We have plenty of examples of different meditations you can choose to do when you wake up. Pick one and do your best to be present. If something makes your mind wander, be open to it, let it pass, and refocus on the practice.

4. **Do yoga.** Yoga is a great way to connect with your body as it is and get in touch with the present moment. It is also a gift you give to yourself by devoting time to increasing the flexibility and strength of the body. In turn, you have increased flexibility and strength of the

mind. It is a wonderful way to start the day. You can do a 15-minute to 90-minute routine and benefit from the time spent.

5. **Take a mindful shower.** There are many things for our senses to feast upon while we take a shower. What does the shower look like? How does the water feel? What is the temperature? How is the pressure? What sounds are you hearing? How does the soap or shampoo smell? What does it feel like in your hands? How does your body feel? Are you relaxed?

6. **Take time to pick out an outfit that you feel good in.** In her book, *Spark Joy,* Marie Kondo invites you to organize and tidy your house by getting rid of any items that do not spark joy in your life. I invite you to do the same thing when picking out an outfit. Give yourself enough time to look at your options. Touch the clothes with your hands and against your body. Smell them. Look at the colors. Do they make a noise that will make you feel uncomfortable? (Think corduroy pants rubbing together!) Choose an outfit that will spark joy, and once you have put that outfit on, reassess whether or not the ensemble makes you feel good.

7. **If you wear cosmetics, mindfully apply your makeup.** If you are anything like me when you apply your makeup (if I put on any makeup), then you are rushing through the process quickly to get to the next task you have to tackle before walking out the door. Slow down the process and do each step with focus and thoughtfulness, and you have a wonderful mindfulness exercise. Each color applied or brushstroke can serve as a way to tune into the present moment. By devoting that time to yourself, you are reinforcing this idea that you are worth it. This exercise will help to clear your mind. When you are done, you will have a finished product you can feel

good about. Not to mention you will start your day feeling more confident and ready to hustle like a boss!

8. **Brush your teeth.** We think of brushing our teeth as one task, but if we break it down into smaller mindful steps, it can be part of our meditative practice. Start by setting the intention to brush your teeth. Listening to the sound of water coming out of the faucet as you wet your toothbrush. Noticing how brushing your teeth feels, and paying attention to how your mouth feels after can all be part of the meditation.

9. **Practice mindful walking.** As you leave your house, you can shift your focus from the list of things that you have to do to what is happening right now. You are walking. It might be from the house to the car or from your apartment to the subway, but until you reach your intended destination you are most likely walking there. As you walk, take the time to pay attention to what is happening in your body. What does your foot feel like when it meets the ground? Can you feel the heel and then the rest of the foot touch the ground? What are your arms doing? Is your body relaxed or tense? What does it sound like when you walk? Is your hair moving? Can you feel a breeze? Pay attention to all of the sensations that are present with openness and curiosity. By doing so you will give your mind a rest, allow it to be more clear, and can start your day from a more centered and aware place.

Mindful Mani/Pedi

One of the regular pleasurable activities I like to engage in is a manicure-pedicure. The hour or two it takes to care for my hands and/or feet is one of the best investments I make in a week or two. It is chock-full of sensory goodness. And guess what? It is not just for the ladies. Some men might be giving me the side eye right now, but some of my metrosexuals and gay men out there already know the pleasure of the mani/pedi. You do not need to get nail polish applied to your finger nails to participate. Maintenance of your hands and feet is a pleasure for all to enjoy.

Enter the nail spot, lounge, spa, or other licensed joint with the intention of being present. Pay attention to what the place looks, smells, and sounds like. If you are applying polish, take time to pick a color that you really like. As the process begins, check in with yourself regularly. What senses are being activated? How does it feel to have your hands or feet massaged? What is it like to have clean and cut or filed nails? How do your hands and feet feel in the water? How do they look? Do all of this while using your breath as an anchor to the present moment. When your mind wanders, you know the drill! And when you are done and have a clear mind, heightened awareness, and fierce or fresh nails, you will be feelin' yourself!

Healthy self-esteem is necessary if you want to have a successful relationship with someone else—or with yourself. Without it you will go through life feeling unfulfilled, resentful, angry, sad, and lonely. If you struggle with confidence, self-respect, or having a balanced view of yourself, it is imperative that you put in the work now and turn that around. You can develop high self-esteem and learn to maintain it despite life's ups and downs. You deserve it.

9 LEARNING SELF-COMPASSION

Imagine a life where you are free to make mistakes, say the wrong thing, walk out of the bathroom with toilet paper hanging out of your pants, have food in your teeth—or do any other thing you can think of without relentless self-criticism. We are so good at self-criticism that we don't even know we are doing it most of the time. But if you begin tuning into your inner monologue, you may soon find out she is incredibly harsh! Every little thing you do is subject to negative commentary. Well, let me tell you that it is possible to change that inner monologue, and that the life you imagined of living comfortably with your own imperfection can become a reality.

Being able to manage your inner monologue can come in particularly handy when you are dating. Dating can be awkward. You could stick your foot in your mouth at some point or do the wrong thing. If you are feeling starved for a relationship, the stakes can be really high. Desperation, low self-worth, and self-criticism can lead to bad choices. Add a negative inner monologue to the equation, and you are in for some painful experiences. To have a satisfying dating life, you need to feel satisfied with yourself and with your life as it is. And to do that, you have to make peace with yourself and your life—and learn how to have compassion for *you*.

WHAT IS SELF-COMPASSION?

Self-compassion is a powerful answer to our habitual self-criticism. It calls for showing yourself kindness when you mess up or are less than perfect. It takes into account that being flawed is built into the human condition, and it allows you to be your whole self and not just the self you want to see yourself as. And, as you might have guessed, it is mindful in nature. Self-compassion involves being nonjudgmental, bringing awareness to the present moment and accepting what is. It helps us to recognize when we are stressed, embarrassed, angry, or having another emotion—and to respond to ourselves with the same empathy and caring that we would show a loved one. Instead of allowing our struggles to make us feel separate from others, self-compassion helps us to feel connected to others, linked by our common experiences. While doing the exercises in this book, you have already started the practice of self-compassion without knowing it. In this chapter we will devote more time to exploring what it is specifically—and how you can apply the principles of self-compassion to your dating experience.

> "Self-compassion is a powerful answer to our habitual self-criticism."

Self-compassion picks up where self-esteem leaves off, according to Dr. Kristin Neff, the author of the book *Self-Compassion*.[1] She sees the pursuit of high self-esteem to be problematic in Western culture because it often means we have to see ourselves as special or above average. Our high self-esteem is only achieved if we are somehow better than those to whom we compare ourselves. This can lead us to avoid looking at our shortcomings. We can become narcissistic if we constantly need to think of ourselves as superior to others.

I believe healthy self-esteem is an important part of feeling good about yourself. Healthy self-esteem does not have to lead to feelings of superiority. You can feel good about yourself while still recognizing the skills, merits, and abilities of those around you.

---

1   Kristin D. Neff, *Self-Compassion* (New York, NY: William Morrow, 2011).

You can do this by practicing self-compassion while developing your own self-esteem. Self-esteem and self-compassion can work together and each can be an asset in your own personal development. When it comes to the practice of mindful dating, self-esteem is not about self-evaluation and comparison to others, but instead it is about building a sense of satisfaction and pride in oneself. This does require that you take your positive attributes into account, but it does not mean that you have to be better than others to accept those traits as good ones.

To find a loving and lasting relationship, most of us have to go through the process of dating. However, seeking love and companionship is pointless if we do not have love for ourselves. To receive love, we have to believe we are deserving of love. Without that belief we are unable to identify a loving relationship, and we sabotage what might be good for us because we are mistrustful or uncomfortable with what is present. Self-compassion teaches us that we are deserving of love, kindness, and acceptance because all human beings are deserving of these inherent rights.

Acceptance and Self-Compassion

Try for a moment to zoom out a bit and focus on others. Think of a friend or acquaintance. Picture that person in your mind's eye. Now zoom back in to yourself, and think of the worst thing you may have said to yourself lately. Got it? Now picture yourself saying that terrible thing to your friend or acquaintance with as much conviction as you said it to yourself. It is hard to imagine doing that, right? If our friend had similar thoughts about themselves we would most likely tell them that they are being hard on themselves and that what they are thinking is not true. We would extend love and kindness toward them. With self-compassion, we can learn how to treat ourselves with the same graciousness we would for a friend, acquaintance, or even a stranger on the street!

It can be pretty challenging to have compassion for yourself when you think you are bad at life. You might believe you

"To receive love, we have to believe we are deserving of love."

are bad at managing your money, bad at expressing yourself, bad at meeting your deadlines, bad at handling your emotions, bad at dating, or a number of other things. Labeling things we do "good" or "bad" sets the scene for us to star in our very own heart-wrenching drama. This happens because of the way we feel about the mistakes we make. For example, if we miss a deadline, we might feel ashamed of our shortcomings. The shame, guilt, or other unpleasant feelings that can be present may lead to attempts to cover up our flaws through isolation, pretending, denial, or being a total poser! None of those options are helpful! An important step toward accepting ourselves as we are is learning how to stop labeling ourselves, and the things we do, as either "good" or "bad." It is not helpful to label our behaviors and ourselves in this way. It does not change the issue at hand. It most likely will complicate the problem because you will lack the clarity of mind to consider possible solutions.

"An important step toward accepting ourselves as we are is learning how to stop labeling ourselves, and the things we do, as either 'good' or 'bad.'"

Acceptance of what is can give you the emotional space to feel what you are feeling about the situation without allowing it to cripple you. Let's take this one step further and add kindness to the picture. You can accept what has happened and how you are feeling while being nice to yourself at the same time. I often get resistance to this concept. There is a sense from people that if you are kind to yourself, then you are excusing the behavior and letting yourself off the hook. There is a difference between being kind to yourself and acting like what you did does not matter. Acceptance of the situation means just that. You accept the whole situation. You accept how your behavior contributed to the problem. You accept the consequences of that behavior. You accept your choices and your role in what has happened. But you do it without beating yourself up. Instead of condemning and judging yourself, you treat yourself with kindness. A little kindness goes a long way when you are struggling. That is why it is our instinct to do it with others. We deserve to bestow that same charitable spirit upon ourselves instead of destroying our self-worth.

Acceptance is the first step toward reconciling with yourself or coming to terms with past transgressions and overcoming personal obstacles. Zen Master Thich Nhat Hanh references reconciliation in his concise guide to relationships, *How To Love*. He says, "If you do not reconcile with yourself, happiness with another person is impossible." Let this idea set in. It is impossible to truly succeed in a relationship if you are in denial or covering up things that you are ashamed of. The foundation of that relationship is built on lies. Lies and shame. That is not the recipe for a healthy and happy relationship.

> "If you do not reconcile with yourself, happiness with another person is impossible."
>
> —Thich Nhat Hanh

DATING FATIGUE

Dating can be a particularly challenging endeavor. You can feel vulnerable, anxious, and unsure of what will happen. Past experiences can linger and give you a bleak outlook on future possibilities. We can be pretty hard on ourselves for dating "failures." Or we can harshly place our dating pool into a box, unfairly labeling it, and let the label give us a negative perspective on the entire experience of dating. Practicing self-compassion while dating can foster a much healthier attitude about the process, making it more enjoyable.

If you are tired of dating and have a negative outlook about the process, you are probably suffering from something called Dating Fatigue (DF). You can find DF all over the internet and PaulBlogs, takes credit for coining the term in 2013. Often associated with online dating, DF is one of those new fangled online terms that basically describes dating burnout. Meaning, you are sick and tired of doing it. You are frustrated by all of the first dates that do not turn into second ones. You are annoyed by having to create the perfect profile. You hate the pressure of having to craft the perfect witty email or text conversation. You are burned out. The most common recommendation for those who are suffering from DF is to take a break. The theory here is that if you can get some distance from all the things you can't stand about dating, then you can later reapproach it with a fresh mind. The only problem with this advice is that you have not addressed the underlying reasons why you have such a negative view of it. There can be value in taking a break from time to time. However, you are doomed to burnout again if you have not learned how your thoughts about dating and yourself are influencing your experience. This is where self-compassion comes into the picture. Adopting a stance of understanding for your challenges or flaws—and taking the time to comfort yourself—can help to ward off the negative thoughts and give you a more positive mindset.

Eight Signs That You Are Suffering from DF

- Whenever you think of dating, you are suddenly overcome with exhaustion.

- You have had one bad date after another.

- You feel annoyed or roll your eyes at your date when he asks you a question.

- You are so cynical that you predict your dates will go badly before they occur.

- The idea of going on one of the dating sites you are signed up for puts you in a bad mood.

- You are way too picky. No one measures up to you expectations, and you can spot a flaw clear across the room before you have even shook hands.

- Your friends are tired of listening to you complain about dating.

- Dating just ain't fun!

Another reason self-compassion is so important to practice while dating is that it helps to foster a happier and healthier you. Without self-compassion, we are at risk of being controlled by our emotions. When we are stuck in our emotions it is hard to be present or emotionally available to others. What do you think happens if you are emotionally unavailable? You do not truly connect with others. You attract other emotionally unavailable people. You do not have the emotional wherewithal to identify warning signs that the person you are with may not be a good fit. And you do not break the cycle of unsuccessful dating that has you so frustrated and is contributing to your DF.

> "Practicing self-compassion while dating can foster a much healthier attitude about the process, making it more enjoyable."

With the understanding and caring approach that is central to self-compassion, you are free to accept things as they are and make appropriate adjustments when necessary. Perhaps your online dating profile is not a true representation of who you are. Maybe you have so many requirements that you are eliminating 99.9 percent of the dating pool. Possibly you need to work on communication skills. Potentially you could be conveying a lack of confidence in yourself that may push others away.

You can learn from things that are happening when your date—without criticizing yourself and sending yourself down a shame spiral. With an open heart and mind you will be more likely to identify what might be contributing to dating difficulties.

CULTIVATION CHALLENGES

Cultivating self-compassion can be quite challenging. One major reason for this is that we have not been socialized to offer ourselves kindness. We live in a culture that is still not very comfortable talking about emotions. In fact, there is a common myth that we all seem to have internalized: you can motivate yourself with self-criticism and by thinking about all of the terrible things that might happen if you do not get your ass in check. This way of thinking has been endorsed by society, and it is reinforced by the short-term benefits you get from using this method. Namely, you jumpstart yourself into action by means of fear and a subsequent adrenaline rush. Remember that fight-or-flight response we talked about earlier? This is what is activated when you motivate yourself with harsh words and negative predictions. However, the long-term consequences of this behavior are plenty. You set yourself up for a never-ending cycle of doing your best to avoid feeling bad about yourself due to the negative monologue playing in your head.

According to neuropsychologist and mediation teacher Dr. Rick Hanson,[2] the brain has a built in "negativity bias" that primes you for avoidance. That bias puts a spotlight on past failures, shortcomings, and loss—and it minimizes current success and abilities. To make it worse, your bias exaggerates future obstacles, making it even more challenging to feel motivated. And so your avoidance, through the means of zoning out or escape, plays a key role in creating more negative thoughts about yourself, only serving as further reinforcement that your thoughts influenced by your negative bias are valid. We think of the thoughts as necessary motivation to get stuff done, but we have gotten it all wrong!

The problem here is that there has not been a real model for how to be nice and understanding to yourself even when you are struggling with difficult emotions—until recently. That is not to say self-compassion was just invented. Obviously, it has been around for a long time. However, due to Dr. Kristin Neff's groundbreaking research and her easy-to-read book about the subject, self-compassion has gotten enough recognition to make it a new hot topic.

---

2   Rick Hanson, PhD, and Richard Mendius, MD, *Buddha's Brain: The Practical Neuroscience of Happiness, Love, and Wisdom* (Oakland, CA: New Harbinger Publications, 2009).

For many of us the idea is completely foreign. When I first learned about self-compassion in 2011, I was convinced that I had been practicing it all along. *Of course, I am kind to myself,* I thought. Next thought, *Oh, I forgot to drop off the preschool applications. I'm such an idiot.* Clearly I had a lot to learn.

Kristin Neff describes it as a moment of revelation when she realized that she had permission to be kind to herself. For me, I was struck with how much I was relying on negative reinforcement and self-criticism to get myself motivated.

> "Even though cultivating self-compassion can be challenging, it is something that everyone can do."

I did it all—comparing myself to others, calling myself names, questioning my self-worth, beating myself up, criticizing myself for having unpleasant emotions, and more. I needed to learn self-compassion. Years later, I am still learning and developing my self-compassion. It is an ongoing practice that I will continue to engage in throughout my life. The incredible benefits include keeping self-worth intact, managing stressful conditions, encouraging the practice of self-love, strengthening resilience, and reducing the impact of tough situations.

Even though cultivating self-compassion can be challenging, it is something that everyone can do. Learning to respond to yourself in a kinder, more understanding way is achievable and certainly worth the effort. As you read this, are you confronted with any negative thoughts about your ability to learn self-compassion? If so, with an open heart, show yourself some love by reminding yourself that new things can be difficult to learn. You have learned other new things that were hard at first, but you got the hang of them. And voila! You have done it! You have practiced self-compassion.

SELF-COMPASSION EXERCISES

"Taildating" Self-Compassion

Who doesn't like a good tailgate? It is the party before the main event. "Taildating" is an uplifting exercise to be done before you go on a date. It will help to foster a state of openness and kindness toward yourself that will be helpful on the date. Put both of your hands on your heart and take three slow and gentle breaths in and out. Now repeat the following. You can do this in your mind or you can say it out loud.

I am starting a new dating journey.

Dating can be challenging.

Challenges are a part of life.

Dating can be fun.

I am open to what this journey will bring to me.

May I be kind to myself throughout this journey.

May I be compassionate toward myself and aware of my needs.

May I be at ease.

Strengthening Our Connection to Self-Compassion

Self-compassion can be hard to access because our minds are wired to have a negativity bias. It naturally looks for problems, either in the past or in the future, when it is at rest. That way of thinking is deeply embedded in our minds, and we automatically fall into those mental grooves created by repeatedly thinking in this way. Think of dirt roads that exist in the woods. They were created by people repeatedly traveling the same pathway. They now look like distinctly carved out routes amidst the trees, bushes, creeks, and twigs, but they were once indecipherable from their surroundings. We must create new mental grooves that strengthen our connection to self-compassion. With repeated practice, those self-compassion pathways will get deeper and will be easier to find—and you will start to naturally fall into them instead of getting lost in the woods.

1. Start by taking a few centering and stabilizing breaths to get in tune with the present moment. Do this until you feel grounded.

2. Pay attention to how you are feeling at this moment. Are you content? Do you feel awkward? Are you hungry? Is there loneliness present? There is no wrong or right feeling. Just bring awareness to what might be present.

3. Now, imagine being with someone who loves you unconditionally. It can be a person, a dog, a teacher. If you cannot identify someone, think of a relationship that you know of, a movie scene, or a storybook where that relationship exists. If you are still stumped, try identifying someone for whom you feel compassion. You want to choose someone that you truly care for. Think of someone you feel "warm and fuzzy" about. This helps you to get in touch with the feeling of compassion.

4. Next, imagine that someone is offering that type of compassion to you. What might that be like? Would you reject it initially? Would you accept it? Acknowledge your automatic response and then open yourself up to receiving that compassion.

5. Next, (and this is often the most difficult part) extend your compassion to yourself. Think of the last unpleasant dating experience or unpleasant interaction with someone you were interested in dating. Be aware of uncomfortable feelings and thoughts associated with that experience. Show goodwill, understanding, and that feeling of compassion you recalled earlier toward yourself. I find doing this while in comfort pose to be very helpful.

6. Acknowledge any desire to move away from this feeling. Instead, take a moment to let it sink in. Bring your attention to the fact that you are receiving compassion and attention. Luxuriously bathe in the feeling of being cared for. Let the feeling penetrate.

7. End by taking a few mindful breaths to bring you back to the here and now, and open your eyes when you are ready.

Self-Compassion Role-Play

Role-play is an effective tool in therapy. It can help people practice doing things they worry about or do not think they are capable of. It can also prepare you to do something that might be hard to remember to do. When we are suffering, self-compassion might be the last thing on our minds. This exercise can help us to integrate the practice into our life through rehearsal. It can be written, performed silently in your mind, or spoken out loud. This exercise incorporates Dr. Kristin Neff's Self-Compassion model.

1. Recall a time when dating caused you suffering.

2. Tune into the feelings associated with that moment.

3. Be mindful that you are experiencing suffering.

4. Acknowledge your common humanity by recognizing that suffering is part of the human condition. Many others can relate to how you are feeling right now. Life can be challenging at times for us all.

5. Extend kindness to yourself. No matter how you contributed to your current suffering or the suffering of others, you deserve kindness. Recognize your role in the situation while showing yourself understanding instead of punishing yourself.

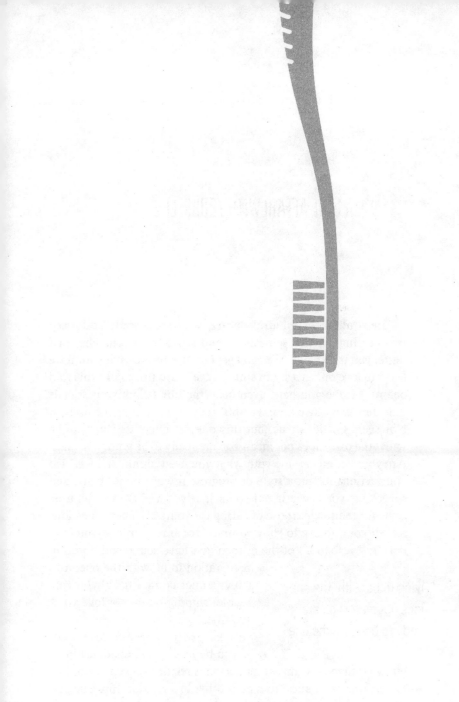

10 A LOVE AFFAIR WITH YOURSELF

In preparation for mindful dating, we have already addressed two key ingredients: self-esteem and self-compassion. The final ingredient is self-love. We can't get our love lives cooking until we learn to love ourselves. I'm sure you've heard things like this said before. Maybe you have even been the one telling your friends that they can't love another until they learn to love themselves. Not every cliché is true, but this one definitely is. Dying to be with "the one" does not mean you are ready to be with "the one." Are your actions in line with what you need, think, and feel? Do your actions reflect a state of progress in your mind, body, and spirit? Are you accepting of yourself as you are? Do you set time aside for the sole purpose of caring for yourself? These questions reflect your ability to show yourself some real love. If you cannot say "yes" to all of them, then you have some work to do in preparation to be with the one. You truly cannot be in a healthy, loving relationship if you do not love yourself first.

"Dying to be with 'the one' does not mean you are ready to be with 'the one.'"

Okay, so you need to love yourself to be in a loving relationship ... but why? One very important reason is relationship conditioning. People take their cues from each other in a relationship. The person you are dating is inadvertently taking in the way you talk about yourself and the way you treat yourself. If you have the habit of mindlessly putting yourself down or saying mean things to yourself when you do something wrong, your partner is gathering this as additional data about you. In time your partner may begin to think of you in the same way—or even treat you the same way—that you treat yourself.

Shira is a twenty-nine-year-old culturally Jewish social worker I have been working with for a few months. She identifies as pansexual, meaning that she is attracted to others regardless of their gender, and she dates cisgender (those whose self-identity is aligned with their biological sex) or transgender men and women. Talk about a large dating pool, right? Her chief complaint was that she could not find a lasting relationship with a good person. She was focused on finding her "better half" and did not feel complete unless she was in a relationship. She reported that all of the people she dated seemed good at first. They were polite, caring, and understanding—all important qualities she seeks in a partner. However, she said that over time they began to treat her poorly. They did not have much consideration for her feelings and were dismissive of her needs. They often began to criticize her and say the things that she thought about herself. These things she thought she was saying in her mind were actually things she was saying out loud. She often complained to her partners when she made a mistake—and when doing so she would call herself names like *stupid, careless, irresponsible, or airhead.* She had a habit of putting things off that she needed to do for herself to prioritize her partner's needs, and she rarely spoke up when she felt she was being mistreated.

Did Shira have a knack for picking people who were manipulative and not forthcoming about who they were at the beginning of the relationship? That was the conclusion she had drawn. Makes sense, right? To a large degree it was probably true. However, the real

Pansexual: attraction and openness to dating others with out limitations of gender, gender identity and biological sex.

Cisgender: a person whose self-identity is aligned with their biological sex.

contributing factor in most of these relationships was her lack of love for herself. In many ways, she was conditioning the people she was dating to treat her in the same way she treated herself. They became disrespectful, judgmental, dismissive, and they lacked empathy for her in the same way she disrespected, judged, dismissed, and lacked empathy for herself.

Shira was not ready to see her role in this dynamic when we first began to explore it in therapy. Shortly after therapy started she began dating a woman she was really into. She was smart, beautiful, confident, caring, and compassionate. She was in her late thirties and had a lot of dating experience, and Shira was extremely attracted to her. Things seemed to start out well. They connected early and spent every day with each other. This one seemed different. She did not put Shira down, or disregard her needs. But after a couple of months ... she broke up with Shira. The main reason she ended things was that it broke her heart to see Shira treat herself so poorly—and that she did not think it was healthy for her to take on the role of therapist or caretaker in the relationship. Shira was used to being broken up with, but none had offered her that kind of insight into why the relationship was ending. It became clear to her that she had to make some real changes and learn how to show herself some real love. In therapy, we learned to identify, evaluate, and respond to the automatic thoughts that were contributing to her behavior, incorporated several new behavioral skills, and conducted several behavioral experiments. We also introduced mindfulness skills, like mindful breathing, acceptance, and being nonjudgmental. In time Shira made a great deal of progress toward her goal of learning self-love.

Like Shira, many of us believe that there is a perfect soulmate out there who will complete us. Nothing could be farther from the truth. There is no better half out there. Thinking of finding someone who is better than you so you can feel complete leads to only one conclusion: you are not good enough on your own. You need another person to fill a void inside of you and make you valuable. Approaching any relationship with that kind of distorted thinking reeks of desperation—and leads to a clingy, dependent, and generally unhealthy connection.

There is a huge difference between wanting a partner and needing one. Unlike needing to be in a relationship, coming from a place of want implies a sense of worthiness. If I *want* a delicious chocolate chip cookie, I might make note of it and make plans to have dessert and indulge in a moist, chewy, chocolatey cookie with my husband on date night. If I need to have a chocolate chip cookie, I will probably mindlessly leave my house and go BCakeNY, purchase a dozen giant cookies, bring them home, mindlessly stuff my face, and then proceed to hate and shame myself for my behavior. Similarly, if you are influenced by wanting a relationship, you are positioning yourself to find love that is based on compatibility, mutual interests, and shared goals. With need as the driving force, you are likely to end up in whatever relationship comes along—just so you have a warm body to fill *the position.*

"The practice of self-love is directly related to the kind of mate you will choose for yourself."

The practice of self-love is directly related to the kind of mate you will choose for yourself. If you think you are unworthy of love and need a relationship to prove that you are, then what kind of a partner do you think you will attract? Often, you will attract those who do not think you are worthy of love either, and they will treat you accordingly. If you believe you are desirable and valuable, you will likely attract people who see those qualities in you. Your beliefs about yourself and how you should be treated will be understood and incorporated by your partner, whether those beliefs are positive or negative. By treating yourself with respect and care and learning to advocate for yourself in a relationship, your partner will learn to do the same.

Learning mindfulness has been pivotal for so many of my clients who struggled with self-loathing. Dating is the process of finding someone you truly connect with. All relationships are about making connections. Mothers bond with their children. Cousins relate to cousins. Classmates join together in common experiences. Friends share and form a bond with each other. Each of these relationships grows and develops through the connection that is formed and nurtured. However, the most important relationship of all is your relationship with yourself. Feeling disconnected and unhappy with yourself makes it virtually impossible to form a true connection with someone else. Think about it. You are sitting there on a date with someone you are really interested in. You want to make a good impression, but you know that you won't because all you can think about are the many flaws you have. He says something to you, but you are tuned out because you are focused on yourself. The exchange between the two of you is labored and disingenuous because you are not even there. To make a connection with someone, you have to at least show up to the date both physically and mentally. Mindfulness practice can teach you how to remain present in the face of unpleasant thoughts and emotions and to be accepting of your flaws.

The principles of mindfulness—self-compassion, non-judgment, and acceptance—are loving by nature. Practicing mindfulness is an act of self-love. The ability to provide loving acceptance and validation to yourself becomes more natural over time. Without the self-love that evolves from being mindful, you will likely fall into a pattern of seeking approval and love from others.

"Practicing mindfulness is an act of self-love."

Have you ever been in a relationship and lost touch with yourself? I have witnessed this with friends and clients—and in the past I have felt lost myself. More recently I have experienced friends who are one way when they are single and a completely different way when they are dating someone. It is as if they become someone else when they meet a person they are really into. They take on their partner's characteristics and interests, and they ditch all the things they once loved to do. It is as though they are shapeshifters, and the longer they stay in the relationship, the more they lose touch with their former lives, friends, and sense of self.

If you are so willing to sacrifice yourself and your current relationships to be with someone, then you are missing the point. Healthy romantic relationships are reciprocal. You give a little; you get a little. You share what you like; they share what they like.

You do what interests him; he does what interests you. You spend a night out with her friends; she spends the night out with your friends. The more you stop doing all the stuff you used to enjoy doing, the closer you get to selling your soul to your partner and losing all of the special things that made you ... you!

A little self-love can go a long way in helping you to stay connected with yourself—no matter who you are dating. With self-love you can make a more sensible decision about whether someone is worthy of your time, energy and affection. The assessment will be based on what you want and need and on what the potential partner is bringing to the table.

Another benefit of having love for yourself is that your increased understanding of how to care for and listen to your needs gives you the insight necessary to communicate those needs with others. When you place others ahead of yourself and do not honor what is in your best interest, you may find that you begin to feel resentful. Without a self-love practice, it is hard to know what you need to communicate with others because you have not invested time in learning about your own needs. You might even tell yourself that if you were important to them they would simply know what you need and take care of you. Self-love teaches you that your needs are just as important as anyone else's needs; it empowers you to be able to speak up about those needs. It takes dedication and effort to get in touch with who you are and to cultivate a loving relationship with yourself, but it is a worthwhile, ongoing pursuit that will help you throughout your life.

DATE YOURSELF!

Do you enjoy spending quality time with yourself? If the answer is not an emphatic "yes," then how in the world can you expect anyone else to enjoy spending time with you? That is why I suggest you date yourself as a way of starting a love affair with yourself. By taking the time to get to know yourself while doing things that are enjoyable and fun, you will learn that your happiness does not have to be dependent on being with others. You will discover that being alone and being lonely are not the same thing—and that you can find joy and fulfillment in the time you spend by yourself. In doing so, you will learn to appreciate the things that you provide for yourself and delight in your own company. The end result will be more chances for you to truly connect with others in a genuine way—and better opportunities to find a relationship that is reciprocal and satisfying.

This assignment will help you to discover the answer to some very important questions: What are your likes and dislikes? What is important to you? How does it feel to be cared for? What are your values? What makes you feel content? Where do you feel most yourself? And many more. Learning these things helps you to bring that awareness of self on a date, which allows you to begin the process of making an authentic connection with someone based on mutual experiences and interactions. This kind of bond can create a pleasurable and lasting relationship and can help you to identify if there is not a multilevel attraction.

No matter what your circumstances are, if you are struggling with being loving toward yourself, you can benefit from "solo dating." If you have trouble connecting with others, attract the same character over and over again, feel unsatisfied in a relationship, have just ended a long-term relationship through a breakup or divorce—or have never had a relationship at all—you can improve your relationship with yourself, and that will have a ripple effect on your relationship with others.

Dating yourself is a way for you to become more mindful of how you are feeling, what is going on in your mind and why you might behave in a certain way. You will be taking the time to discover yourself—and because you are doing so in a nonjudgmental and compassionate way, you will uncover the real you. Being in tune with these parts of yourself opens you up to being your most radiant, sexy, confident, and attractive self. You see yourself as worthy, a goddess, a divine being—and you recognize your magic within. Confidence is the most attractive quality that anyone can possess.

So here are the steps to dating yourself. Now, you may be doing some of these things already. If so, then I want you to start doing them with the intention of loving and caring for your needs and gaining a new sense of awareness of yourself. Remember to be kind to yourself in the same way you would be to a child who is learning something new. As with any new skill, this will take time.

Step 1: Set time aside to date yourself by scheduling it in. Give yourself the same courtesy you would expect from a suitor and plan in advance. You have a busy life, filled with many things on your to-do list. Make this a priority.

Step 2: Decide what you are going to do with that time. A date can range in activity. You might decide to cook yourself a nice meal, take a hike, go to a play, check out a new restaurant, take up a hobby or activity you have been interested in, go to the spa, or attend a local book talk. The most important thing to consider is whether the activity is of interest to you and whether or not it is something you want to do. It could be helpful to think of things that you might like to do with a friend or loved one and plan to do that activity by yourself. Also, never underestimate the importance of doing nothing from time to time. Some of the best dates are the ones where nothing is planned and you just go with the flow.

Step 3: Engage in dating prep. Why should you only spend time getting all dolled up for someone else? Do the same routine you might do in preparation for going on a partner date. Here are some examples of what you might do to get ready for your solo date: Shave your legs because it makes you feel sexy to have super soft, silky legs. Spend time picking out a nice outfit that is activity-appropriate and that you will feel attractive in. Wear sexy underwear. Put on music while getting ready. Apply make-up and perfume or cologne. Get your hair done. Make sure to highlight your assets. If you have a nice ass, put it on display in a nice pair of form-fitting jeans—or if you have a great smile, make sure to flash those pearly whites. You get the point!

Step 4: Go on the date with mindful presence. Take time to check in with yourself regularly and get in touch with what is happening in the moment. Note what is enjoyable and what is less enjoyable. Observe your thinking from time to time. Be open to the experience, and enjoy the moment.

Step 5: Touch yourself. This can go as far as you would like for it to go. For some, buying a new lotion and applying it to yourself is enough. For others, buying a new vibrator and caressing yourself is good. Do what feels good to you, but show yourself tenderness and love through touch.

Step 6: Reflect. Take some time to think over the date. What was it like? How did you feel? What did you like? Would you do it again? What would you do differently next time? I recommend that you do this by formally journaling about the experience. Taking the time to do so is loving in nature, and it will help to reinforce the activities of the evening.

Loving-Kindness Meditation

Now what better way to deepen your love affair with yourself than with a loving-kindness meditation? This type of meditation strengthens self-love by cultivating feelings of love, compassion, kindness, and empathy toward both others and ourselves. It has been proven to increase our well-being by boosting positive emotions like joy, contentment, pride, hope, and gratitude. It is also associated with decreasing symptoms associated with many mental health and physical disorders. It helps you to connect with others by providing you with a more positive outlook. Finally, it decreases your self-criticism, resulting in an improved relationship with yourself.

You start this meditation with an openness to the experience and a willingness to be the benefactor and recipient of love, kindness, and compassion. Set this as your intention, and allow yourself to be open to what should be present throughout the meditation.

We begin by closing our eyes and breathing mindfully until we feel present and grounded. Once we are ready, we extend loving-kindness to ourselves first because, as we have discussed, loving others starts with loving ourselves.

There are many variations to this meditation. Here is one I like to use:

May I be filled with loving-kindness.

May I be accepting of my whole being.

May I find joy.

May I have ease of body and mind.

May I be at peace.

Repeat the phrase several times. Let the words sink in, and allow them to wash over you. If you find it difficult to do this, picture yourself as a child. Say the words to your child self. Do not worry if it feels awkward at first. That is normal. It will take practice for it to feel more natural. Continue to say the phrases until you are truly receiving them. This may take about five minutes.

Next, extend the phrases to someone in your life who has inspired you. This could mean different things to different people. It might be a teacher, friend, or family member who has shown you a great deal of care and support. It could be a public figure whose work you admire. As long as it is someone whom you see as a benefactor, the meditation below will work well. Now, picture that person in your mind's eye and repeat the following:

May you be filled with loving-kindness.

May you be accepting of your whole being.

May you find joy.

May you have ease of body and mind.

May you be at peace.

Repeat the phrase several times. Keep the vision of your benefactor in your mind's eye. Continue to bestow loving-kindness upon them. Feel the gratitude you have for them in your heart.

When you feel you are ready, move on to your loved ones. Picture them in your mind and say the following:

May you be filled with loving-kindness.

May you be accepting of your whole being.

May you find joy.

May you have ease of body and mind.

May you be at peace.

Repeat this several times while allowing your feelings of love and support to come to the surface. It is okay if the images change, or if people come to mind who you were not expecting. Be with what is, and continue to open your heart.

When you feel you can move on, think of the neutral people in your life. This could include the clerk at the bodega you go to in the morning, the security people at your office, your UPS carrier or anyone else whom you interact with during the course of the day. Imagine you are looking at them and say:

May you be filled with loving-kindness.

May you be accepting of your whole being.

May you find joy.

May you have ease of body and mind.

May you be at peace.

When you are ready to move on, think of those who may be suffering. They might be physically or mentally ill. They may be having financial difficulties. Perhaps they are separated from their families. Think of who that might be and how deserving they are of love, kindness, and compassion. Picture yourself giving them a gift. That gift is your loving-kindness toward them. Repeat the phrase:

May you be filled with loving-kindness.

May you be accepting of your whole being.

May you find joy.

May you have ease of body and mind.

May you be at peace.

In time, when you feel you can transition to the final granting of loving-kindness, think of the difficult people in your life. It might be someone who has hurt you. Perhaps it is someone who has not taken responsibility for what they have done to violate your boundaries. See them clearly in your mind and repeat:

May you be filled with loving-kindness.

May you be accepting of your whole being.

May you find joy.

May you have ease of body and mind.

May you be at peace.

When you are done, open your eyes and take note of how you feel. Is the feeling pleasant, unpleasant, or neutral? Do not worry if you had difficulty the first time. Just keep at the practice. Your wish for goodwill, peace, and well-being for yourself and others is one of the purest forms of love. Your willingness to give it to others and to yourself is invaluable and will help to create the foundation to receive love from yourself and others.

TUNE IN TO YOUR LOVING INNER MONOLOGUE

We have talked about how often our inner monologue can be focused on the negative. Your faults, flaws, and mistakes are easy to access, and there can seem like no shortage of material for the inner voice to draw from. However, with a little practice, we can start to change the discussion and steer it to a more productive and loving spokesperson. The idea here is to engage in dialogue with your compassionate and loving self. Your loving inner monologue's purpose is to give you the love, compassion, and understanding that you deserve simply for being alive. By repeating the identified statement below, you will develop a mind-body connection as you begin to recognize the link between the warmth and love you are feeling and what you are saying.

This exercise is a great way to start your day. I recommend you do it after you wake up, perhaps while you sit with your morning cup of tea or coffee. Take a few mindful breaths in and out to ground yourself and be present with what is happening in the here and now. In your mind or out loud say, "I love you, and I want the best for you." Repeat this for a few minutes. With practice you will begin to feel connected to what you are saying. In time your loving inner monologue will come up with some new encouraging and loving statements on its own because it has been primed.

You might become aware of thoughts like, "You are strong," "I forgive you," "This difficult time will pass," "I love you," and "Keep up the good work."

Once you have cultivated a loving relationship with yourself, you will be equipped with some of the basic tools you need to date mindfully. You will gain a better sense of self and of what is important to you. You will have an improved quality of life that is independent of external validation. You will develop an increased ability to be intimate and communicate with others, and you will have improved decision-making skills based on your needs and desires. Not to mention you will feel a whole lot better being who you are.

PART FOUR
PRACTICING MINDFUL DATING

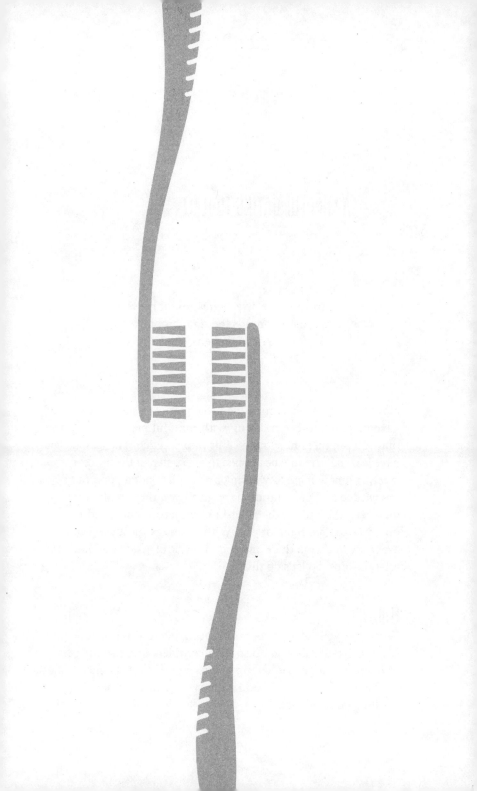

11 A MINDFUL DATING TOOLKIT

> Any guy can sweep any girl off her feet;
> he just needs the right broom.
> —Alex Hitchens, *Hitch*

Now that you have learned the principles of mindful dating and have prepared to begin dating with mindful presence, it is time that you put these newfound skills into practice. The lessons you have learned can now be applied to every step of the process from meeting a new mate to walking away if it is not a good fit. Your knowledge and preparation have given you the foundation to go out there and attract the right kind of person and weed out the ones who are not right for you. With openness and awareness, you are ready to get out there and end the cycle of disastrous dates and relationships. So let's do this!

FLIRTING

Flirting is your way of communicating interest in someone, and it is important that you do so with confidence or else the person of interest will get the wrong message or not get the message at all. I have said it before, and I will say it again: confidence is your sexiest characteristic.

You might be thinking to yourself, *But I am shy!* I want you to observe that thought. Accept it for what it is, and then refocus on the task at hand here: dating! It's time to act in the face of discomfort if you want to get some results here. You have to take charge of your destiny—and flirting while shy can be charming and flattering.

So how do you flirt while projecting a sense of confidence and not seeming needy? Here are some ideas:

- Flirt in the moment. The most important tip, of course, is to be mindful. Flirting has to be done in the present moment. People will be attracted to your ability to interact and respond to what is happening in the here and now, and you will have an easier time making a connection.
- Use your body. Believe it or not, Disney's *The Little Mermaid* has some important nuggets of truth that we can apply here. Ursula the Sea Witch was an evil, manipulative ... well, witch, but she did give the naïve and misguided mermaid Ariel some sound advice: "Don't underestimate the importance of body language. Ha!" Make sure you are projecting openness by keeping your arms uncrossed and your body facing the person of interest. Listen to your mom's old advice, and stop slouching! Good posture communicates that you are comfortable in your skin, helps you to feel more confident, and makes you look slimmer and more proportioned! And look your new crush in the eye. Don't stare him down like you are a Matador about to conquer a raging bull, but do look at him as you are talking. (A little trick is to look back and forth every couple of blinks to keep yourself from staring—and to add a little sparkle to your eye as the light is reflected differently with movement.)
- Summon your loving inner monologue. Your self-love practice will come in handy here. Remember some of the loving thoughts that have surfaced in response to

your increased love for yourself. Some examples might be, "I love you," "You are amazing," "I am proud of you," or "I am likeable." If you cannot come up with any on your own, feel free to use these examples. The idea is to remind yourself that you are worthy, unique, and loveable. Doing so puts you in a positive mind space and gives you that extra boost you need to mingle. Let everybody see the most fabulous version of yourself. Need some inspiration? Turn on the beats and listen to Nicki Minaj and Beyoncé's "Feeling Myself."

• Get handsy. When it comes to flirting this is one time when you do not want to keep your hands to yourself. *Subtle* touching shows that you are interested and creates a physical connection. Now, don't get all creepy and cross any boundaries here. Most people do not want you to get up in their personal space without an invitation. Try this instead: Lightly brush the back of his hand with the back of yours and see if there are any sparks. Reach across the table to touch his hand. Touch his shoulder as you tell a witty story. But make sure you are aware of how he is reacting to your touch. Be mindful of whether he pulls away or changes the subject. This might be a sign that he is not interested. But if he makes eye contact and smiles, leans in, or grabs your hand, then you are probably in, baby!

WHERE TO SEEK YOUR SOULMATE

Now that you have some ideas about how to show interest and attract a partner, let's talk about where you can find those who are ripe for the pickin'. The truth is, you can meet "the one" anywhere. When you are engaged in what you are naturally doing, it can make for a more authentic exchange with someone you meet. But I do think that if you are in the partner-searching biz, it is important to note that there are definitely some places that are better than others.

You might have heard that bars or clubs are not a great place to meet people. There are some compelling arguments for why that is true. For one reason, everyone might be drunk! Yeah, that might make striking up a conversation easier, but the content of that conversation is probably not going to be all that interesting if you are both wasted! Also, you are in an environment where most people are looking to hook up and have a good time—and not necessarily start a relationship. Don't forget that there is a ton of competition, and with competition comes game-playing. How do you get that guy to notice you? What do you need to say to keep him interested? How can you manipulate the situation to work in your favor? The point here is to find a soulmate, not to trick someone into liking you!

It is important to be aware of the possibilities in all environments. But you have to get out there. Unlike a casting call or a talent show, thousands of eligible suitors are not going to show up dying to go on a date with you. You have to go out there and locate the likely lovers. But where? Like I said, the best place to find a partner is in places you already enjoy going to. This shared interest is a good way to initially connect and can help to get the party started. Are you still scratching your head trying to think of where you can go? Here are some ideas:

The Gym. Talk about a place that is swarming with single folks. The gym is a great place to meet someone because you are all there for the same reason: to take care of yourself. If you are in a routine you are likely to see some familiar faces after a while. That familiarity can go a long way in making you feel comfortable approaching someone. Keep in mind that there are a lot of people who go to the gym ready to bang out a quick workout. So if someone is not quite as receptive to you it could be because they are extra focused on a goal, have a family to go home to—or a number of other possible reasons.

Unsure of how to start a conversation at the gym? Try:

- I've seen you here a few times. Do you work around here?
- I've heard the machine you are working on is really

good for your core, but I am a little intimidated. Could you show me how to use it?
- You are in great shape! Have you worked with any of the personal trainers here? I've been thinking of getting one.

The Grocery Store. My mother was never quite into dating after she broke up with my sister's father in her early thirties. But she was (and still is) quite beautiful and was always getting picked up. I remember her often coming home from the grocery store and telling me about some guy who was trying to put the moves on her. Many years later I came to realize why the grocery store was such a hot meat market. Single people gotta eat too! Yes, some of them order in from GrubHub or Seamless regularly, but they have to make their way into a grocery store at some point to get a few essentials. There are plenty of singles who do cook—and who doesn't like a partner that cooks? Keep some of these things in mind while shopping for the catch of the day:

- The checkout line is a great place to start up conversation—because what the hell else do you have going on? There are plenty of things to chat it up about. If they are looking through gossip magazines or a *Yoga Journal* you already have a topic to talk about. If the line is long you can make a joke about it. Or if you see something interesting in their cart, you can ask about it.
- Are you looking for the kind of partner who shops for food at a Walmart Supercenter or Whole Foods? Identify the kind of person you are looking for, and shop at the corresponding grocery store.
- Keep in mind the neighborhood you tend to shop in. Yeah, the grocery store close to work is convenient, comfortable and you know where everything is … but if it is in the West Village and you are straight, you might be limiting your pool of eligible talent.
- When is prime shopping time to find a mate at the grocery store? Millennials have set the trend to have a

much more flexible schedule with their nonconformist work-at-home lifestyles. But the vast majority of us still work a 9–5-ish job, so shopping will most likely occur in the evening. So strolling around the market at 6:00 p.m. could be a good idea.

- See a hot prospect while you are in the personal hygiene aisle? Please wait! Make eye contact, and then wait to see what direction they head in—and meet them in the next aisle. Conversation over the tampon of choice is no way to start a relationship!

Sporting Events. You love the Brooklyn Nets. Why not look for a fellow fan where the action is? Arenas, stadiums, and other sports venues are swarming with single folks. Emotions are running high, and there is already a sense of camaraderie and familiarity among those on the same team. You can show off your passion and knowledge or ask questions to a fan who will be more than happy to show off himself. Here are some possible obstacles you might encounter that you can overcome:

- He's hot, but he's rooting for the opposite team. That's a deal breaker, right? Not necessarily. A little flirtatious trash talk can go a long way, and you might feel some passion ignite between the two of you as you defend the virtues of your teams.
- Tickets are expensive! Yes, that is true if you want to see behind the dugout (or practically anywhere else) at Yankee Stadium. But wait, you can become one of the Bleacher Creatures for a fraction of the cost. Yes, you are farther away from the action, but that doesn't mean you can't roam around the stadium and check out the fan candy.
- He's with a group of people. Okay, that can be intimidating for even the most confident of us ... but a group of people shouldn't get in the way of finding your true love! Situate yourself close to the group and try to make eye contact with someone you might be

interested in. If that doesn't work, hang tight. A single chick all by herself is sure to get someone's attention. He's not doing it for you? Ask about who he's with, and see if that gets you an introduction into his posse.

Coffee Shops. Feel like getting some coffee? Guess what, so does everybody else! That is why there is a Starbucks on every other city block. All you non-coffee drinkers are in luck too. They have tea, hot chocolate, apple cider, smoothies, and ice creamy shake-like drinks with whipped cream on top.

In the romantic comedy classic *You've Got Mail*, Joe Fox makes the brilliant yet somewhat judgmental observation that "The whole purpose of places like Starbucks is for people with no decision-making ability whatsoever to make six decisions just to buy one cup of coffee. Short, tall, light, dark, caf, decaf, low-fat, non-fat, etc. So people who don't know what the hell they're doing or who on earth they are can, for only $2.95, get not just a cup of coffee but an absolutely defining sense of self: Tall. Decaf. Cappuccino." (Oh, how I long for the days of anything at Starbucks costing $2.95!) As funny as that statement is, I think it misses an obvious point for my single folks. There is a lot of information to be gathered from what a person orders, and you can use that information as a way to engage someone in a conversation. "Tall, Decaf, Cappuccino? I would have never have thought to order a Cappuccino decaf? Is it any good?"

A coffee shop is a logical place to socialize, but not one that most people take advantage of. Perhaps this is because you might think you will feel awkward or vulnerable. That may be true, but you do plenty of things that are outside your comfort zone when you see the value in doing them. So let me shed some light on why the coffee shop is a good place to meet other singles. First, you have a large influx of people coming in and out, and opportunities abound. Second, people tend to have a coffee routine, and that can be a way for you to "run into" someone who might have caught your eye. And finally, you won't seem like a creepy stalker because there are plenty of other folks there people-watching and chatting. The environment is less threatening and meat market-like, so you are not as likely to be viewed as predatory.

All you need is a killer strategy:

- Find a good spot in the shop where you can be social. This is a very integral piece of advice. Your natural inclination might find you heading toward a table in the back corner where things are less hectic ... but that is not where the action is. You have a few key places to situate yourself so that you can strike up a conversation. The front door allows you to make eye contact, give a smile, or even verbally greet people as they enter. A seat by the coffee retrieval area is a great place to strike up a conversation because people are waiting around for their drinks with nothing to do except stare at their smartphones. The communal table or other areas where seats are facing each other gives you a natural common space where you can easily connect with others.
- Ask about or comment on what they are drinking, eating, reading, etc. This is a perfectly logical thing to be interested in if you are sitting near someone who really seems to be enjoying what they are doing at the moment.
- Use people-watching to your advantage. Look over at the person you have your eye on, and ask them if they think the couple across from you guys is on a first date? Talk about how, for example, you couldn't help but notice the awkwardness of their not knowing each other combined with the excitement present between the two of them.
- Get the advice of a cute guy in line behind you. This is the perfect chance to see if he has anything to share that could help you find your next favorite beverage— and in doing so, you might make a connection.

Take a class. What better place to meet people with similar interests than in a class where you are both learning something new.

You will be surrounded by others who are trying something new, and this is a great way to connect with others. Bonus: you might be able to get a study group together and get to know your person of interest on a deeper level. So what kind of class should you consider? Here are some tried and true suggestions:

- Continuing education courses are a great way to invest in yourself—and a good way to meet someone doing the same thing. Whether it is something that will help to advance your career (like a computer course) or something to feed your soul (like Intro to Italian), you can express your passion for it to a fellow student who might share your enthusiasm. Let the sparks fly! Worst-case scenario, your resume is a little more padded, and you will be able to hold your own when you go on that trip to Tuscany that you have been dreaming about.

- A wine tasting might not exactly be a class, but you are learning something new and have a chance to discuss wine with someone discovering the same thing. You like wine; he likes wine. You are already off to a good start. Now strike up a conversation about the notes of the wine and what it might be good paired with. Like his suggestion? Perhaps you could invite him to try it out with you over dinner.

- Cooking class is a wonderful way to strengthen your mindful eating and cooking practice and to meet new people. There are plenty of classes to choose from, and luckily for you there just happen to be classes devoted to cooking for one person. Find this class, sign up, and get to socializing. You are sure to find a single person of interest in there—and if not, that can work for you too. Surrounded by other single women and you are looking for some man candy? Chat these other women up, and see if they have any single guy friends. Perhaps you guys can combine your newfound skills and have a dinner party, invite your single guy friends and see if there are any matches to be made!

Online. We cannot talk about dating and leave out the most-used source of finding a date today. Online dating is no longer for the socially awkward or people who cannot get a date on their own merits. (Not that is ever truly was, but that is the stigma that seemed to be attached to it.) Nowadays, online dating is how it is done—and if you are ignoring this powerful tool, then you are doing yourself a big disservice. There are a multitude of sites to choose from, from the really popular Match, Tinder, Grinder, EHarmony, Plenty of Fish, Zoosk and OKCupid!, to the more specifically tailored FarmersOnly, PinkCupid, BlackPeopleMeet, JDate, BeNaughty, ChristianMingle, and OurTime. There is a particular kind of dating site for whatever you are interested in, from lifestyle and ethnicity to age and religion. If you are new to online dating and share some of the prejudices about the process, it is time for a serious attitude adjustment. Get with the times! If you are not new to online dating but are feeling frustrated and burned out, you can reenergize yourself. Here are some tips:

- Don't be so wordy. Whether it is your profile or an email to a person of interest, say what you mean to say and then be on your way. If you are funny, be funny. If you are flirty, be flirty. If you are smart, be smart. But for goodness sake, do not *try* to be any of these things. You will be identified as a poser, and your connection will be lost. There is no need to fret over each little word choice and to spend time constructing the perfect response. Just be genuine and hit "done" or "send."

  Ghosting: The act of suddenly ending a relationship by cutting off all communication (phone call, texts, emails, unfriending you, etc.) with no explanation.

- Be up front about lack of interest. This goes for any kind of dating but seems to be a particular problem for online dating, perhaps because the relationship is founded on what some may perceive as a less personal face-to-face way of dating. However, ghosting someone is not cool. Especially when you seem to be interested, are investing time in the person, and making future plans. If you start to become aware that you are just not that into him anymore, let him know. It won't be the most pleasant conversation, but it is the right choice for people with integrity and human decency!

- There are a lot of weirdos out there (on- and offline). Don't be one of them. It is very easy to be misunderstood when you are communicating in written form because tone can be hard to decode. You do not want to sound like a creep, so make sure to dial down the flirtation. That is not to say you shouldn't be flirty. Just make sure there is some balance there—and that you are not coming on too strong or aggressively.

- Be yourself. Yes, you can find a way to be your most attractive and confident self online, but make sure you are being a better version of yourself and not selling people a phony representation. If you are kinky, skinny, and white, and you are interacting with someone looking for a sexually vanilla, curvy Latina … don't pretend you are J-Lo with a "plain" yet healthy sexual appetite. No one deserves to be catfished!

Catfish: To entice and lure someone online into a relationship by pretending to be someone else. Usually, the persona is fictional.

- Choose the right photographs for your profile. People who seem personable are the ones who get the most action online. That is why it is helpful to put up pictures with friends or pets you love. Also, try to stay away from using that really gorgeous picture of yourself from the last wedding you attended, or that sexy Halloween costume you wore last year. Casual, approachable, and attractive is the way to go.

- See if there is something there. Do not dismiss people because they say they are "laid-back," and you know your type A personality will not mesh with theirs.

People are notoriously bad at identifying their characteristics. I have had a quite a few people laugh in my face when I have described myself as laid-back. I tend to react by taking offense, overreacting, and then vowing to prove just how laid-back I am! Okay, I guess I am not laid-back... How I see myself and how others see me is quite different. This is true for most of us. Wait to make a judgment on someone's personality traits until you actually spend some time with them. But use those mindfulness skills to suss out personality in their profile. You are sure to get a sense of someone by the way they express themselves if you are consistent. For example, sarcasm is hard to hide if that is part of the natural way you communicate with people.

Some other hot spots you might want to keep in your back pocket: the dog park, bookstores, yoga studios, museum tours, running and biking clubs, dance class, networking events, gallery openings, beer-making class, bowling and shuffleboard leagues, religious events, and volunteering opportunities, to name a few.

Reality Check

Putting yourself in the environment and striking up a conversation is simply not enough anymore. If you are interested in someone and think there is a real possible connection there, you have to step up and make the first move. Whether you are male or female is no longer important. Old school gender roles keep us stuck because that is not the world we live in anymore. Ask your person of interest out. If he says no, it might sting— but at least you do not have to live with the regret of a missed opportunity, and you know you have the balls to go after what you want.

WHAT TO DO WHEN YOU SCORE THE FIRST DATE

Pick a Good Place

First dates are all about finding a connection, so it is important that you pick somewhere to go that will allow for you to do just that. The movies are a typical first-date option, but why the heck would you choose to do something that does not involve talking or getting to know each other? Save that one for later on when words are not needed. Restaurants are another popular choice, but they can make for awkward dates if you find yourself stumped for things to talk about or feel like you are being interviewed for a job. Instead, think of places where you can be active with the environment while connecting with your date. Walking and talking can make for some good conversation because you are engaging with what is happening around. Or perhaps you can choose a fun activity where you both have to work together or challenge each other. Something interesting to talk about is sure to come out of some good teamwork or healthy rivalry. Some great ideas for walking and talking first dates include the museum, the botanical garden, the park, the zoo, and a walk over a bridge. Some great ideas for an active date are indoor rock climbing, bowling, shuffleboard, table tennis and roller- or ice-skating.

Dating tip: Connect on a deeper level. Compliment their abilities—not superficial things like their appearance.

Order Something Delicious and Enjoy It

Food can help you be mindful of what is happening in the here and now. If you are enjoying your meal, you have something to talk about and perhaps share with your date. Food can be a great way of connecting. He will also get a glimpse into your passion for life and things that you enjoy. Just make sure you choose something that is not messy and will not get stuck in your teeth. You might want to pass on the BBQ ribs for the first date.

Be Open with Your Feelings and Thoughts

The whole point of a first date is to get to know each other. How are you going to do that if you are holding back your true feelings? Sharing your feelings and thoughts makes you human and helps to facilitate a connection between the two of you. If you are enjoying yourself, say so. If you think he is handsome, tell him. If he is slaying you with one joke after another and you are loving it, own that! When you are comfortable with who you are—and willing to be vulnerable—you are also making room for your date to do the same. He is getting to see the real you. The open, sexy, feeling, passionate version of you is attractive and worth sharing.

Put Your Phone Away

There is nothing more annoying than being out with someone who is constantly checking their phone. Believe me, I know. My husband is an on-a-date-phone-checker! He only gets a pass because we started dating in the pre-mobile phone era. But if you pull this move on a first date, you are sure to turn your date off. It shows that you are more interested in texting someone else than you are in the person you are with. Way to win her over, right? No one wants to feel like they are being cheated on with a phone when they are on the first date.

Drink in Moderation

Sloppy drunk is not a good look. But it is surprisingly easy to find that you have crossed that line on a first date. You might want to seem game. Like you can hang with the big boys and girls. Or you could just be feeling uncomfortable, and you think that drinking will help you to come out of your shell. Or perhaps there is no thought behind it. You just keep throwing back one after another without any awareness. So you keep drinking until you reach the point of no return. That is not the vibe you are trying to give off. It is in the complete opposite spirit of mindful dating because being drunk robs you of your ability to make choices based on what is happening in the here and now. Have a drink or two if you can handle it, but if not, skip the drink and get drunk on love instead.

Stay Present

I hope this one goes without saying. If not, this book has been an epic fail, and you should chuck it into the fire ASAP. But just to add a bit more emphasis, I will humor you with a little reminder to stay present. It is in this moment that you have the opportunity to find a true connection. So make the most of it and tune into to what is happening in the here and now.

Now, if your date happens to bring up the future and wants to discuss it, I say proceed with caution. You can engage him in a conversation about the future, but don't use this as an opportunity to unload all of the plans that you have for him or to interrogate him about his family planning goals. Be cool. Be breezy. Let the conversation flow, and stay in the moment.

Notice you are losing touch with the present moment?

Try mindful hydration. Take a look at your glass of water. Notice the frost or condensation, the ice, and the size of the glass. Is the water clear? Do you have a lemon wedge in there? Touch the glass. How does it feel? What is the temperature? Bring the glass to your mouth. Do you hear the ice clinking or popping? Did a ring hit against the glass and make a noise? Is your body reacting to the anticipation of drinking the water? Taste the water. How does it taste? How does your body react? Now look up into your date's eyes, and focus on what is happening in the moment.

Get Your Flirt On

Now that you are a flirting expert, you need to put your skills to the test. If you are into your date, make sure he knows it with a little harmless flirting. If you are doing it right, he will get the message—and you will feel like a powerful sex goddess. Make sure to pay attention to his flirt game. If you are like me, you will be sure to miss it if you are not mindful of it. I mean a guy or gal could ask me out for coffee after telling me how beautiful I am, and I would still think how sweet they were for wanting to be my friend. That is, until I use mindfulness to intentionally pay more attention to the signals. Turn on your flirt radar, and make sure you are showing that you are attracted to your date.

Don't Bring Up Exes

This is a rookie mistake that happens way more than it should. It is only natural to want to know about who your date has been with, but that sets the table for him to ask you the same—and then you are both engaged in a conversation of ex-bashing. That is not cute. Or perhaps it goes a different direction, and he learns about how wonderful your ex is—and now he is comparing himself. Your ex has nothing to do with the date you are on now. Past relationships are in the past. Keep them there. If things go well, there will be plenty of time to get to know about each other's previous romances. And if not, it was none of his business anyway!

Turn Down for What? Just Go with It!

Adam Sandler is my favorite rom com leading man. Okay, I love him in almost anything! But in rom coms in particular, he shows us the importance of going after what you want.

If you like him, let him know! Have some boundaries, of course, but throw the arbitrary ones out the window. If a kiss feels right, let it happen. The spontaneity, newness, and excitement of a first kiss can create a bond between the two of you and make the wait for date number two a thrill. If your date seems shy, make sure to initiate physical intimacy in a way that feels comfortable and appropriate to you. That might look like you grabbing your date's hand, looking him in the eye, saying how much fun you had, and kissing him on the cheek. Or if you're a gangsta, you might plant a big wet one on him without waiting for him to make the move. Let your mindful presence inform you about what feels right.

If you didn't feel any immediate sparks, try to be optimistic. First dates can be awkward. If your date is feeling nervous or insecure, you may not be able to get a real sense of the person you are with. It is hard to know someone from one encounter. Try a second date to make sure there really isn't anything there.

If you are sure this is not going to work, listen to your gut and be up front. Leaving people in the dark when it comes to dating might seem appealing because you get to avoid unpleasant emotions and prevent a negative reaction, but it is cruel and selfish to do so. Make the choice that has integrity, and be honest about how you are feeling. You can say something like, "It was really nice to meet you, but I don't think we are a good romantic match." Simple, to the point, and clear.

SECOND DATES AND BEYOND

You got a second date? Score! Time to pick out a drawer in his dresser for your toothbrush and extra clothes, right? Hold up! You are still getting to know each other. You guys may be off to a great start, but if you rush things, you may end up on the fast track to splitsville. It is always a good practice to take your time when you are getting to know someone you are interested in. Remember those boundaries you learned to identify and set? They are still important to keep in mind. It may feel good to spend every waking moment with this new person, but you have to maintain a sense of self and continue to live your life while getting to know them.

Be mindful of your need to rush, control, or force things, and then put yourself in check. You are trying to build something here. Here are some things to keep in mind:

Allow Courting to Happen Naturally

You may have had a great first date and want to keep the ball rolling, but is it necessary for you to take on that role? We are certainly living in different times, and gender roles are being challenged ... but in heterosexual relationships, a lot of men still want to be the one doing the chasing. It activates the "natural" male instinct to hunt, and the chase is exciting and fun. So when women take the initiative, it could feel emasculating for some guys. In addition, you rob yourself of the opportunity to see if this guy has any balls. By doing all the work for him, you never get to see if he was interested enough to do it himself. If you have been the one making all the moves and are unhappy with your dating life, it might be time to employ this old-fashioned method and see where it gets you. This does not mean that you cannot express interest and say you would like to see him again. Please do those things. Just maybe hold off on taking charge and setting up the next three dates.

Slow It Down

Sexual attraction can be hard to deny. So why should you deny yourself the carnal pleasure of getting it on? Answer me this: How many long-term relationships have you had with people whom you slept with early on in the relationship? Sex can be amazing and fun. But it can also trick you into feeling closer to that person because of the love hormone oxytocin, which is released when you have sex. It is the same hormone that is released when you breastfeed your child, and it can be quite powerful—but it is not based on a true connection. When you slow things down sexually, you allow for a true connection to develop based on mutual interests, attraction, values, and respect.

Desperate Is Not Appealing

It is important to have a strong sense of your own value when you start dating a new person. This is why I spent so much time

Thirsty: So desperate for love that you go after a partner just like you might go after a drink of water after running a marathon in 90-degree weather.

discussing how to develop your self-esteem. When you know your worth you will present as confident—and confidence is very sexy. Needy and desperate is the opposite of sexy. When your value is in question, you may come off as way too "thirsty." Dating can be inherently scary and test your sense of worth. You are just as good as he is. Know that, and wear it with pride. Without knowing your worth, you will certainly lose sight of your authentic self—and remember, the goal here is to find a real connection by being genuine.

Don't Use Him for Free Therapy

He might be a great listener. You might feel like you can open up to him. Don't do it. He is not your therapist. He is a date. You should not use date time to emotionally process your issues. In fact, why are you talking about your problems with him anyway? Save all of that for much later on down the line when you two have really gotten to know each other and there is something substantial there. Even then, do not get into the habit of dumping on your partner. It is not his responsibility to solve your problems.

This is not about withholding information. It is about waiting to share intimate parts of your life until things are more intimate in your relationship. Your family drama or inability to pass up eating an entire pizza when you are feeling vulnerable is not beginning-of-the-relationship material. Seriously, save it for your therapist. If this sounds like you and you do not have a therapist, start your search right now.

Leave Him Wanting More

I am definitely not into playing games when it comes to relationships, but I do think that it is important to have a mindful presence when it comes to how much time you are spending with someone as you get to know them. If you spend too much time, you send the message that this is all you have going on in your life right now. And that could not be further from the truth. You have a full life, and he should see that so he can get excited about how he can be a part of it.

Also, if you give up all of your time and everything there is to know about you in the beginning, then there is little left to discover as you embark on this relationship. It is a good thing to have limits on the amount of time you will devote to a date. It allows for you to build excitement. It leaves him wanting more. It gives you more to discuss the next time. This will help to keep things fresh and progressing.

Safety First

Things might be going well … really well. You might feel as if you have known him for years. Well, wake up! You haven't! You have known him for a few encounters. That is not enough time to know whether he is well intentioned. Remain cautious, and set clear boundaries around your safety. Meet in public places instead of having him pick you up from your place. He does not need to know where you live yet. If something does not feel right, then pay attention to that. Remember, I want you to be open and start building trust, but that does not mean that you jump right into a relationship and give him full access to everything in your life. That comes with time and is earned. Be mindful of what you are sensing, and let that awareness inform your decisions.

DEVELOPING A HEALTHY RELATIONSHIP

You are in luck! A lot of what we have been working on up until now will lend itself nicely to building a healthy partnership. You have set the stage to be your authentic self and to have a trusting relationship. You know your self-worth and have worked on being less needy. You have found someone who connects with who you genuinely are, and you have in turn connected with someone based on more than just superficial qualities or potential. So how do you build on this great start?

Good relationships are nurtured. You work at maintaining and developing them by investing time and energy into them. Just because it is good now does not mean it will remain that way. It is unrealistic to expect things to continue to be good if you are neglecting your partner. Here are some important things to keep in mind as you go from just dating to becoming a couple:

Teach Your Partner Your Boundaries

Now that things have moved into a more serious stage of your relationship, it is important that you continue to uphold the boundaries that you have identified are necessary for you to feel comfortable and secure. You do this by openly communicating your needs, defining what is comfortable and what is not, and reinforcing it when a boundary is crossed. Oftentimes, people are unaware that they may be crossing a boundary until they are told about it. Some may even forget about it and cross that boundary again. However, if they are respectful of your needs, they will be invested in learning how to make you feel safe and understood.

When you and your partner clearly define your needs and boundaries, you are setting a strong foundation for a relationship. Emotional intimacy will flourish and grow from this nourishing soil composed of openness, clarity, respect, non-judgment, and honesty.

Be Honest

This piece of advice seems to keep coming up a lot, doesn't it? Well, that is not a coincidence. Honesty is important at every stage of your relationship. You must be honest with yourself. Are you still attracted to this person? Do you feel safe with them? Do you feel respected? Do you have similar life goals? Are you both headed in the same direction? You must be honest with your partner. What are your thoughts, dreams, goals, feelings, and desires? Be aware of things you may be holding back—and why. If you do not feel comfortable being honest, understand that this is a problem and address it with your partner.

It is important that you encourage your partner to be honest as well. If there is something that you do not understand or that is concerning about your partner's behavior, ask him about it. Stay away from that old pattern of reading his mind and assuming that you know what is true. That does not set the stage for an honest exchange.

Take Responsibility

Couples fight, and people make mistakes. It is bound to happen. When it does, you need to put on your big girl Spanx and ask how you contributed to the situation. If the problem is clearly your fault, own up to it. If it is a little more complicated and you had a role in the conflict, make sure you take responsibility for your part in it. The way you take responsibility (or don't) says a lot about your character. It is nearly impossible to feel good about yourself if you do not act with integrity. Be the person you want to be—even when it is hard—and you will get far more out of your relationship.

Fight Fair

Fighting does not define a relationship, but the way you fight can. Learn to settle conflict in a fair way. If you are too heated to fight fair, wait until you have cooled down. Be careful of the things you say. People have a tendency to pop off at the mouth when they are angry, hurt, or threatened. Once those words are out there, you cannot take them back. A great tool for expressing yourself when there is a conflict is the "feedback wheel" as developed and explained by author, speaker, and family therapist Terrence Real.[1] It helps you to take responsibility for your thoughts, feelings, needs, and actions—in addition to keeping you on topic.

The steps of the feedback wheel are relatively simple. First, you express what you heard or saw happen. Keep it factual, and do

---

1 Terrence Real, *The New Rules of Marriage* (New York, NY: Ballantine Books, 2007).

not add in your opinion. Second, share what you thought about the situation. In doing so, make sure you use "I" statements. "I thought you didn't respect me." "I believed you were not being honest." Third, state how you feel about the situation and your subsequent thoughts. "I feel hurt, insecure, and angry." Finally, tell your partner what you would like to happen in the future. Share your needs. Be clear and honest about what change you would like to see.

This method is useful and effective for many reasons. It is non-blaming. It is direct. It is open. Most importantly, it is mature. You are taking responsibility for your own needs. You are not holding your partner responsible for guessing what your needs are and then punishing them when the fall short. This is an adult way of handling conflict that can bring about real change.

Have Compassion for Your Partner

When you learned how to have more compassion for yourself, we discussed how it is much easier to have compassion for others than it is to have it for ourselves. The exception to that rule is when it comes to your partner. Over time you can begin to direct some of those same rigid, unforgiving, judgmental, and unkind thoughts you have about yourself toward your partner—or for your relationship as a whole. Cultivate compassion for your partner, and you will become more open and understanding of your relationship. As you become less judgmental and approach your partner with kindness, you will make room to respond to situations in a more balanced and helpful way.

WHEN IT'S TIME TO CALL IT QUITS

As Boyz II Men sang, "It's so hard, to say goodbye to yesterday." But if things are not working for you, it is time to go. So, how do you know when to let go of a relationship? You guys are together for a reason, right? You had so much in common and were so connected to each other. How can you walk away from that? Sometimes it will be clear that a relationship is over, and the struggle will be less about knowing when to end and more about knowing *how* to end it. Other times you may be ambivalent—or even afraid of letting go. Here are some signs that it is time to move on.

You What Now?

No one is completely open and honest when you first start dating. There may be certain things that you conceal because they are deeply personal and you are just getting to know the person. Or maybe there is something about you that you find embarrassing, and you don't want to feel judged. That is normal and human. But if you and your new boyfriend are doing great and you are really starting to fall for him, and suddenly he drops a serious bomb on you ... that can be hard to reconcile.

Imagine he nonchalantly shares that he has three children he never mentioned. Or that he has a crazy ex-girlfriend who is vengeful and takes her anger out on the new girlfriend ... you! When someone you are dating reveals something he was not up front about, it can create some serious trust issues. The truth is you have to know your boundaries—and if the revelation crosses one, makes you feel uncomfortable, or is unacceptable and in direct conflict with your goals or needs—it is time to walk away.

I Can't Stand the Sound of His Breathing

There used to be a lot of great qualities that you could identify about your partner. He was sweet, a good listener, a great lover, funny, charming, and really talented. But nowadays all you notice are his ever-present, irritating behaviors. He leaves his clothes everywhere. Or he chews with his mouth open. Or worst of all, he breathes too freakin' loud! Minor annoyances have taken over your consciousness. And they become

Dating tip: Use your skills of awareness. You can learn about how your date treats people by the way he treats your waitress. Pay attention.

more and more pronounced to the point that you can't stand being around him anymore.

When this happens it is time to take stock of the relationship. Is there something here to hold on to? If there is, then it is time to work on it with your partner—or maybe even in couples counseling. However, if you truly have checked out of the relationship and are simply tolerating him so you can have a warm body next to you or a date to the next wedding you are invited to, then it is time to say buh-bye!

He Said He Would Stop

Oftentimes we turn a blind eye to warning signs early on in a relationship. We want to see the good in people, and we may be more in tune with our desire to couple up than we are with the actual person we are coupling up with. It is my hope that you are able to identify this before you are actually engaged in a partnership. But if one has slipped through the cracks, then don't beat yourself up. Instead make the choice that is in your best interest.

Perhaps when you met you two were single and partying often. He liked to drink and recreationally use drugs, and it never seemed to bother you. But now it is starting to take a toll on the relationship. He is more interested in partying than in being responsible and upholding his role in the relationship. Or maybe he seemed passionate in the beginning of the relationship and you really liked that. But over time his passion took on a more aggressive turn, and you are uncomfortable with his actions toward you. You have told him how you felt, and he has said that he would stop … but nothing is changing. Accept what is in front of your eyes. He is not going to change. It is time to cut your losses and hit the road.

No Trust

Both people suffer when trust has been broken in a relationship. If you have been hurt, you are in constant state of high alert— most likely looking for more examples of how your partner is untrustworthy. You are angry and in pain, and you may find you cannot connect to your partner anymore because you believe he is a deceptive, manipulative person with hidden motives. The one who has done the hurtful thing feels guilt and judgment from their partner. There is discomfort, defensiveness, and a sense of hopelessness. This is a lot for any relationship to endure.

Trust can be rebuilt over time. If you are both committed to making the relationship work and are invested in doing what it takes to create a trusting relationship again, then a healthy relationship is possible once again. Be mindful of whether you have it in your heart to work toward forgiveness, letting go, and moving on. If not, be honest with yourself and your partner, and end things so you can both start over again with someone else.

You Want Different Things

As a relationship develops, certain things are put on the table that may not have been discussed in the beginning. Yes, you are vaguely aware that you both have similar family goals and have a lot in common … but what about when some fundamental differences in lifestyle are revealed?

You may learn that your partner has a problem with his finances that directly affects your planning for the future. Or maybe his family plans to come to visit for months at a time, and you are not down with that. What if you are accepting of each other's different religious views, but one of you is set on raising your future kids with your religion? It is time to look at how important your beliefs are compared to your partner's and see if there is any room to compromise. If there is not, use your best Arnold Schwarzenegger impression because it is time to say, "*Hasta la vista, baby.*"

Breaking Up Is Hard to Do

No one likes to break up with someone or be the person who is getting dumped. That is why there are so many stories of people ghosting each other. This practice has become all too popular over the past five years or so as online dating has gotten to be more popular and communication via the means of texting, email, and social media have become more commonplace. Perhaps it is because our devices have handicapped our communication skills and made it easier to go off the grid with a swipe to the left, which in turn has made us more callous. Or maybe we are just too afraid to do what is difficult. However, no matter how hard it is, it is important when you end a relationship to treat the other person with respect. Be mindful of your values, and act in accordance with them. Here are some things to consider in your approach:

- Be direct. You can be honest and forthcoming without being cruel. The truth may be that you have found him increasingly annoying over time and you are no longer sexually attracted to him ... but you do not have say all that. Instead, tell him that you have grown apart and are no longer feeling the same way about him as you did in the beginning.
- Don't just blurt it out. Think about what you want to say and how you want to say it. It could even be helpful to do a role-play with a friend. Be thoughtful in your approach and genuine in your intentions. Remember this was once someone you cared for deeply.
- Do it in person. Carrie from *Sex and the City* was famously broken up with by Burger on a Post It. How pathetic and cowardly is that? Well, the modern equivalent of the Post It break up is the text breakup. Don't be a coward. Unless you feel you are in danger, be brave and talk to your partner face to face. Just to be clear, emails, phone calls, social media, and faxes are not acceptable either. Unless you happen to be in a long-distance relationship and will not see each other for a long time, respect your partner, the relationship, and yourself by getting closure in the flesh.
- Anticipate they will have some feelings about it. It hurts to be rejected, even if you know things are not going well. So it is important to be understanding when your partner reacts to your ending things. He may say hurt-

ful things or walk away as if nothing happened. Let him have his reaction and be willing to listen and swallow your pride. Unless, of course, you are in any danger. Then you have my permission to run for your life!

- If you have found someone else, own up to it. This can be the scariest thing of all to do. Yes, it can be extremely hurtful for your partner to hear. However, he will find out eventually—and when he does, the hurt will be multiplied because you were not honest in the first place. Do your best to tell him in a kind way, but be upfront.

Got Dumped?

Chances are, if you are willing to be vulnerable enough to date, you will encounter someone who does not see the same potential in a future with you as you do with them. I know, I know: it is hard to believe that someone won't see how fabulous you are. But heck, even Jennifer Aniston got dumped by Brad Pitt! And don't get me started on Taylor Swift. Half of her music catalog would not exist without her experiences of being broken up with. Breaking up is hard to do, but being rejected can be even more difficult. That is why it is important for you to keep these things in mind:

- **Mourn.** It is normal to be upset when you are rejected. Let yourself experience the full range of emotions that come along with it. If you ignore or deny your feelings, they will make themselves known in ways that you do not have control over and will regret later on!
- **Cut off all ties.** I am not saying that you cannot be friends with an ex, but that will come in time, if at all. For now, it is important for you to separate yourself from the relationship so you can start to heal and move on. So, no more texting, booty calls, social media connections, social media stalking, or calling his mom to check up on him.

- **Do not hold on to the pain and the anger.** You may need to vent to a friend or family member from time to time but it does not do you any good to stay stuck in your resentment. When you allow yourself to let go your unpleasant feelings, you open up the possibility for more pleasant and positive experiences. Remember, bitter does not look good on anyone!
- **Thank your lucky stars.** It may be hard to see it now, but getting dumped was the best thing that could have happened to you. It was not meant to be. And now that it is over, you can look forward to finding someone who is truly a good fit. Even if you were dating *People Magazine*'s 2016 Sexiest Man Alive, Dwayne "The Rock" Johnson and he kicked you to the curb, it is important for you to recognize that although he seemed perfect, he was *not* perfect for you. So, be grateful that you still have the chance to find the one who is perfect for you.
- **Get back to *you*.** After you have given yourself the time you need to mourn, let go of the unpleasant feelings, and be grateful for your new opportunity to find a better match. Focus your energy back on the most important person of all: YOU! Get back into the things that make you who you are. Enjoy time with friends, go to the gym, cook your favorite meals, get a makeover, watch your favorite movies, and play all of your favorite Backstreet Boys songs and dance naked in your bedroom to them...or whatever rocks your boat.

No matter what dating stage you are in, you now have some useful tools and strategies that incorporate all that you have learned. The mindfulness principles of non-judgment, openness, and awareness of emotions, thoughts, and behaviors applied to dating make for a more genuine connection with your date—but also with yourself. Always remember that you have a responsibility to yourself to uphold your standards of self-care, self-love, self-compassion, and self-respect. If you date within those parameters you will find your experience will be much more satisfying.

12 MINDFUL MATING

Ever since we said 'I do,'
there are so many things we don't.
—Ricky Ricardo, *I Love Lucy*

Warning: This chapter includes racy
language meant for grown folk!

Does sensual, romantic, throbbing, pleasurable sex sound good to you? It does to me! Who does not want to have a rich, fun, and exciting sex life? And sex between people who care for each other and are deeply connected is pretty hard to beat. That is a big part of what we are seeking in a soulmate. So once you have snagged that love interest, what is the formula for a hot sex life? A lot of folks think of it simply: Mutual attraction plus desire plus arousal = hot carnal pleasure. In fact, Dr. Helen Singer Kaplan's model of sexual response states that desire, arousal, orgasm, and resolution is the normal pathway.[1] But sometimes it is not that simple. There

---

1   Helen Singer Kaplan and Melvin Horwith, *The Evaluation of Sexual Disorders: Psychological and Medial Aspects (New York: Brunner/Mazel, 1983).*

are other pieces to the puzzle that may be missing or underdeveloped. Sex is not just about the body or the genitals. Yes, they are important, but the biggest sex organ we have is the brain. What is happening in our minds is just as—if not more—important than how wet we are or how hard we get. Sex is said to be about friction and fantasy. And where does fantasy happen? In the mind of course! This is where mindfulness comes in handy!

WHAT IS MINDFUL MATING?

By now you have a strong sense of how mindfulness can enrich your life. We have looked at how it can transform your relationship with yourself, others, and the way you interact with the world. Mindfulness allows you to respond to any situation with awareness and openness, thus giving you more opportunity to act authentically. Mindful mating is the practice of having sex while embodying this nonjudgmental awareness of your thoughts, your feelings, and what is happening in your body. This means that you don't categorize your sexual experiences as "good" or "bad." It also means that you do not try to change the way you are feeling. This frees you up to see what is, and truly connect with your partner in the here and now. Sex becomes a total mind-and-body experience that is much more pleasurable and meaningful. Sounds good, huh?

Let's explore this more.

Sexuality is an important part of who we are. It is part of what makes us human, and it is our natural birthright to engage in and enjoy sex. Because we are sexually repressed as a society, we do not often talk about sex in a way that supports these truths. However, we cannot deny the influence of the daily messages in the media that are given to us about what sex is and should be. Complicating things, there is not enough talk about all of the different things that sex can be. So if we think of sex as anything other than a man

Sex: The physical act of touching, kissing, and stimulating yourself and a partner. This act includes oral, anal, and manual stimulation of genitals, in addition to sexual intercourse or penetration.

and a woman in missionary position having intercourse until they both climax at the same time, we tend to feel isolated, abnormal, or ashamed. Sex is so much more than that.

Unfortunately, we are also extremely orgasm-centered when it comes to sex. We get so far ahead of ourselves during sex that we focus only on the destination and miss the entire journey along the way. There is enjoyment in that journey. There is pleasure in the moments that lead up to orgasm—if an orgasm even occurs. All of it is worth experiencing. Mindfulness helps you tune into every moment and increase the pleasure.

A key component to having good sex is learning to be comfortable in your own body. Your body is a temple to be appreciated, adored, and cared for. You do not have to possess washboard abs, giant breasts, or a thick, long, and rock-hard penis to feel good about yourself. We all have what we perceive to be flaws and fall short of our ideas of perfection. Self-acceptance is one of the greatest gifts you can give to yourself. It frees your mind from constant self-criticism and makes room for your loving inner monologue to speak.

Awareness is a fundamental element of mindfulness in sex. In this case, I am referring to awareness of what you want and do not want sexually. What are you into? What turns you on? What parts of your body are erotically charged? What parts do not feel good when touched? Do you like dirty talk? Are you into BDSM? Do you have conservative sexual tastes? Do you like to incorporate toys? There are so many things to get to know about your own sexuality.

I once went to a sex-education professional development event that included a trip to a BDSM club. They shut down the club and made the visit very hands-on and experiential for our group of therapists, sexual educators, and nurse practitioners. I tried being flogged (whipped) by the Dominate/Master (fully clothed of course!) and found it to be extremely pleasurable. My typical sexually vanilla ass never thought that I would find flogging to be a turn-on—yet I discovered that my sexuality is still evolving, and yours may be too. Learning more about yourself, being aware of and in tune with what you want and do not want, makes it possible for you to communicate your wishes to your partner—and to set boundaries that provide you with a sense of comfort.

WHEN TO HAVE SEX

Comfort is another important part of having enjoyable sex. Your partner should be someone you feel safe with. When you are at ease with your lover, you are able to surrender to the experience. Sexual pleasure is very much about surrender. Can you control yourself into having an orgasm? If you tell yourself, "Have an orgasm" over and over again, you are actually more likely to prevent it from happening. That is because you are trying to force it to happen. I see this with my sex therapy clients often. Some are so focused on making that orgasm happen that they are unable to be vulnerable with their partner and thus prevent it from ever happening. Letting go of control and giving in makes the experience more erotic and satisfying. But it is hard to do that if you do not feel comfortable with your partner. This is why some people advocate waiting until you get to truly know your partner. Comfort and trust develop over time. If there is potential for trust to grow but it is not quite there, it is probably in your best interest to wait before you become sexually intimate.

Another reason to consider taking your time before you become sexual with a new partner is the love hormone, oxytocin, which is released during sex. Oxytocin may give you a false sense of closeness to your partner. Mothers release it when they are breastfeeding, and it is even thought to be exchanged

BDSM (Bondage and Discipline/Dominance, Sadism and Masochism): A set of erotic practices involving roleplaying sexual expressions. Though there are gray areas, common roles include a dominant and a submissive or master and slave. The motto "Safe, Sane, and Consensual" denotes there are clear boundaries in place and well-being is built into the practice.

"The real foundation for a loving and lasting sex life with a long-term partner is a connection at a deeper level."

when people give a meaningful hug. So if you have sex early on in the relationship, you might trick yourself into feeling like you are in love and deeply connected with the person—even though you haven't really developed those feelings or that bond yet. The real foundation for a loving and lasting sex life with a long-term partner is a connection at a deeper level. Emotional and spiritual closeness can lead to a hot sex life because you two are able to communicate verbally and nonverbally. You are able to be in tune with what gives you and your partner pleasure, and you can pick up on the nonverbal cues that help you to really connect. This kind of communication provides you with a way to be much more intimate.

There is no magical amount of time that you must wait before you have sex with someone you are hoping to have a long-term relationship with. It can be different from couple to couple. For some folks, waiting until they are married is what they believe in, and I am not going to judge that decision any more than I am going to judge people who start knockin' dem boots on the first date. However, I do want for you to be mindful and consider waiting until you have comfort, safety, and a true emotional and spiritual connection. If you have a pattern of sleeping with partners early on and it does not seem to convert into longer-term relationships, then perhaps you should try taking a more mindful approach and waiting until you have real closeness based on trust, emotional intimacy, and a strong sense of who your partner is.

SEX KILLERS

One thing mindfulness and sex have in common is that they both reduce stress. However, stress is a major mood killer and can make being sexual really difficult. So how can you use sex to help reduce stress if you are too stressed to have sex? Mindfulness is one powerful way to do so. It helps to reduce suffering through acceptance of what is and gratitude for what we have. It will help you to get some spaciousness around your stressors and relate to them in a more adaptive way. And this can make room for you to enjoy sex more—and reap the benefits of it as a stress management tool.

Another sex killer is a preoccupation with your body. Sex is a mind-body experience. It is impossible to be in your body if you are stuck in your head. Few things kill hot sex more than someone who is worried about how they look or what their partner is thinking. If you are focused on how your breasts look hanging over the sides of your body, how many rolls you have in your gut, or how big your ass looks ... you are not in the moment. Or if your mind is preoccupied with thoughts about being judged by your partner or doing something wrong in sack, then you are missing out on the action. Sex is about feeling and connecting. The feeling of your partner's soft mouth on your inner thigh can be electrifying. The potential for pleasure in that moment is abundant as you anticipate where he will put his mouth and tongue next. The possibilities are not just in that body part—but all over. The hair on your arms might stand up, your nipples might get hard, you may get wet and more. But if you are preoccupied with worries about him noticing your cellulite, you will undoubtedly miss out on that sensual moment.

That is not to say a thought won't pop into your mind. But when that happens this is the time to employ some of those mindfulness and CBT skills of acceptance and acknowledgment. Be aware of the thought as just an idea. Allow it to pass, and refocus yourself on what is happening in the moment. Get out of your head and into your body.

SEXUAL ENERGY

There is a certain kind of energy that courses through you when your sexuality is activated. When you and another person are engaged in a sexual exchange, that energy can be a powerful charge that transcends both of you. This typically only happens when there is deep loving connection between the partners. There is an emotional presence that serves as a conductor for the energy to flow. Your hearts are engaged and connected, creating a pathway to something greater than yourself.

I recently heard two different kinds of people talk about sex. One was a Catholic conservative, overachieving young man. The other was a sex educator and sexual surrogate who teaches people with sexual difficulties to get in touch with and own their sexuality by being sexually intimate with them at times. One had very restrictive views about sex, and the other had very expansive views. However both described sex between two people in almost the same exact way. They talked about there being a trinity of sorts, where there is a connection between partner A, partner B, and a deep spiritual presence. They spoke of sex transcending the two people, joining them as one and creating a new spiritual state of being. It is that energy and closeness that facilitates this kind of sexual experience. This is the potential of your sexual intimacy with a partner that you are truly connected to.

SEX AND THOUGHTS

It is normal for your mind to wander while you do anything. Sex is no different. You might be thinking about how you look or if you are pleasing your lover. You could be replaying in your mind the scenes from the latest porn you watched. Or maybe your thoughts are completely unrelated to sex and you are worrying about a meeting you have tomorrow, or how you are going to make it in time to pick up the kids. Whatever kinds of thoughts you are having, they are distracting you from being with and enjoying your partner.

"Spectatoring is the act of watching yourself perform sexually instead of being a part of what is happening."

"Spectatoring" is the act of watching yourself perform sexually instead of being a part of what is happening. When you are more focused on how you look or how well you are performing, you are no longer connected to your partner, and you become an observer instead of an active participant. This mindless activity kills intimacy and makes enjoying sex infinitely more difficult than it has to be.

Things can take an even more difficult turn if you start to worry about whether you are going to be able to perform or come. Concern about pregnancy or STDs can also steal the focus and take a starring role in your sex life. This is especially true if this kind of thinking becomes habitual and you develop an association between your worries and sex. For example, a man who is overly concerned about whether he will be able to get and maintain an erection can form an association between sex and worry that can develop into erectile dysfunction. If you are preoccupied with worry, you are not connected to what is happening presently in your mind and your body—and sex is all about what is happening in the present moment.

MINDFUL MATING EXERCISES

Great sex is all about being in the present moment. It is the quintessential mindful experience. This means, among other things, that you need to practice being nonjudgmental, aware of your expectations and open to what is present in the here and now. It also requires you to trust in yourself and your partner, let go of criticisms, and pay attention to all of the sensations that are present. The following erotic exercises range from slightly sexy to totally titillating and are designed to help you get in touch with your sensual self. Get ready to kick the grown-folk talk into high gear!

Sensual Body Scan

Meditation is an effective way of getting in tune with your body and priming yourself for a mindful mating. It gives you an opportunity to witness your thoughts and let them pass while you connect with your sexual being. I like to do this exercise lying down. Much like a body scan, this exercise has you focusing on breathing into and out of body parts. However, the body parts you will be focused on are your sexually erogenous zones, including your genitals, your abdomen, your breasts, your anus, your buttocks, your neck, your feet, your mouth, your ears, and any other body part you can think of. If you have female genitals, try to focus on the parts of your genitals such as your clitoris, vulva, and vagina instead of simply thinking of your vagina as one thing. If you have male genitals, then try to think of the head of your penis, the shaft, and your testicles instead of just your penis as one body part.

Start at your lowest identified erogenous zone on your body and breathe into it. Breathe in passion, desire, energy, and anticipation. As you inhale, imagine that body part receiving the connection, love, and closeness you desire. Breathe out tension, worry, and control. As you exhale, imagine all of your concerns separating from you like soap bubbles that you blow into the air—and watch them drift away until they are no longer visible or until they pop.

Continue moving up your body, repeating the process with each body part until you reach the top. End the body scan with this positive loving thought: *I deserve pleasure, love, connection. I am in my body and am ready to receive and give pleasure, love, and connection.* Repeat this thought as needed. Now you are ready to have a sensual, intimate exchange with your partner.

Abandon Expectations

One way we can really sabotage sex is by having too many expectations about how the experience will be. When we find that the experience does not live up to our expectations, we feel disappointed, defeated, and deflated. There is potential in every sexual encounter, but it is impossible to see that if you have already decided how the encounter is supposed to go. You cannot appreciate the small things because you are focused on the outcome. It is time to recognize if you are doing this and abandon your expectations. Try this exercise to practice letting go.

- Get in a comfortable seated position. Close your eyes. Take five mindful breaths, slowly breathing in through your nose and out through your mouth.
- Continue breathing, and pay attention to any thoughts that come to mind. Acknowledge the thought, accept it simply as an idea, and then let it pass while refocusing on your breath.
- Now repeat the following mantra: "I am a sexual being. I am open to what this encounter may bring

me. I let go of all my expectations." Continue taking mindful breaths while repeating this statement to yourself five to ten times.

- If another thought comes to mind, pay attention to that thought. Acknowledge it, and then let it pass while refocusing on your breath and the mantra.
- When you are ready, close the exercise by taking five more mindful breaths. Open your eyes.

Touch and Be Touched

One of the basic tools we use in sex therapy is an exercise called Sensate Focus. Masters and Johnson created this exercise as a way to build intimacy and trust, develop your sensory awareness, and improve sexual pleasure. You and your partner take turns giving and receiving pleasure through touch. It starts intentionally with non-genital touch, but every other body part is up for grabs, so to speak. Eventually, as you progress through each stage, you end with genital touch and intercourse if that is desired. You each spend a designated amount of time (usually 20–30 minutes) exploring your partner's body with your hands and your mouth. Touching, tickling, lightly squeezing, kissing, and licking are all permitted. As you explore your partner's body, the focus is on giving pleasure—but also on paying attention to how your own body and your partner's body react to your touching. Do you feel aroused when kissing the V on his lower abdomen that leads to his genitals? Has your breathing quickened while caressing his arms and placing his hand on your face? Does his mouth opening softly showing you that he is enjoying your stroke?

The exercise below is similar to the Sensate Focus exercise, but has a slightly different intention. The idea is to enhance your sexual experience by getting you and your partner in tune with each other through nonverbal communication.

- Talk to your partner about wanting to enhance your sensual experience with a new exercise. Explain the benefits and make sure they are on board.

- The next time you two engage in sexual activity, use the Touch and Be Touched method. You do not have to schedule a time to do this because you have already discussed adding this. Once it is clear to you or your partner that sex is going to happen or is on your mind, invite your partner to be touched.
- Both of you may remove your clothing. You may do this on your own or ask for your partner to assist you. If you would like to leave underwear on, do what will help you feel comfortable.
- Have your partner lie down on a bed or couch or comfortable spot on the floor. During your time, explore your partner's body. Make sure not to neglect any body part. Touching their face, feet, fingers, etc., may be much more erotic than anticipated.
- Do not spend too much time on any one body part. Give it ample attention and then move on to the next.
- Pay attention to your partner's response. Are they leaning in? How is their breathing? Is their face relaxed? Do they seem tense? Are they moving away? All of this and more is important information for you to take in and respond to. Remember, the goal is to give pleasure. If something you are doing does not seem pleasurable to your partner, move on to something else.
- Experiment with pressure and varied touching. See how your partner may anticipate your touch. Use your mouth and tongue to explore body parts.
- Engage all of your senses. What are you seeing, hearing, smelling, touching, and tasting? This is not just about touch. It is a total sensory experience.
- Pay attention to what you like about touching your partner.
- When your touching time is up, switch places with your partner and surrender to their touch. Allow yourself to enjoy receiving pleasure. Be open to the

experience. Be curious about your response and your partner's response.

- If something does not feel good, gently move your partner's hand away.
- When your time is up, use that sensory experience and the connection you had with your partner to progress in your sexual play and see where that can take you.
- After sex is done, talk to your partner about the experience. What did you like? What didn't you like? What surprised you? Share what you noticed when touching, and see if your nonverbal communication was clear.

Sex and mindfulness are a natural pairing. A good sexual experience with a partner is all about being in the moment and connected to what is happening in your body and with your partner. Good sex is inherently mindful. You will not regret the time you spend cultivating your mindfulness practice when you see what an amazing impact it can have on the intimate connection between you and your partner. Once you can let go of your expectations, learn to get out of your mind, pay attention to what is happening in the present moment, and enjoy the sensory experience that is sex, you will soon see all that mindful mating has to offer you and your partner. I encourage you to get busy practicing right now!

IN SUMMARY: ESSENTIAL MINDFUL DATING TIPS

In my line of work, I develop groups for people to work on specific areas of their lives. Watching my clients transform over the time we work together is truly satisfying for me as a therapist. I think of these beautiful people as butterflies; to me they are the definition of change, strength, beauty, and potential.

I feel the same way about the readers of this book. Dating isn't always fun and easy; we know it can take a toll on how you view yourself, your possibilities, and your world. As you continue to practice mindful dating and interact with your partners in new and improved ways, you too are going through a transformation. I want to encourage you to pay attention to what has changed and what has the potential to change. I want you to give yourself credit for the work you have put in and the positive adjustments that have occurred. And I want for you to open up to what may still need a little more attention. No matter what stage you are in, I hope you allow yourself to acknowledge your potential and your progress. When you do this, you allow your transformation into a butterfly to occur. Make space for your true self to surface, spread your wings, and fly.

Do you remember as a kid being given the task of connecting the dots? A bunch of meaningless dots on a piece of paper, when connected in the right sequence, can reveal a clear picture and provide us with delight and a sense of accomplishment. As you continue to work on your mindfulness practice and employ the skills we have addressed, I believe the picture will become clear to you as you take each new step and connect each dot. Here are my dots: my tips and reminders for keeping up your practice.

- Practice mindfulness! The benefits of meditation, yoga, or many other mindful activities are beyond words to describe. By cultivating awareness and living in the present moment, you give yourself a choice instead of moving through life on autopilot. Mindfulness is an effective practice in relieving countless problems. It reduces anxiety and stress, helps you alleviate depression symptoms, increases your capacity for pleasure, and strengthens relationships. Regularly practicing mindfulness will give you the tools you need to make the most of any date you are on, helping you to remain more present. Remember, to find a true connection you must be your most authentic self. If you are not present, then you are not able to be yourself. How can a genuine and long-lasting relationship begin if you haven't even shown up for the date? It can't. Case closed!
- Have an open mind and heart when it comes to dating. So many of us have a list of arbitrary attributes that a partner *must* have to be considered an appropriate suitor. Or perhaps we think we are entitled to love and that it will magically come to us. Or maybe we rush into sleeping with people we really like and confuse sex with love. These and other dating devices can lead to us away from connection and make us miss out on a great person and a wonderful relationship. Open up to new possibilities and you may find that some of your requirements and old behaviors belong in the past.
- Be aware of distorted thoughts about dating. Mission Cognition is fully underway! A mindfulness practice includes being aware of the habitual ideas you may have that are unhelpful. We all have them, but

you must be aware of what thoughts you are prone to in particular and be curious about how they might be holding you back. One technique I like to use is to follow these steps: (A) Identify a warped thought. (B) Breathe in, repeating the thought. (C) Breathe out, asking, "Am I sure?" This exercise gives you the opportunity to accept the statement at face value or challenge it. How true or helpful are statements like, "All the good ones are taken," "No one is ever attracted to me" or "There is no way he will like me after seeing that lipstick on my teeth." Those thoughts are unproductive and unkind.

- Don't be too critical of your date. You are just getting to know each other. To be mindful, you must practice having a thought and not judging it as "good" or "bad." You are simply observing the thought and letting it pass. The same is true when you are dating. People do and say things on those first dates that they would not normally do or say because they are nervous, insecure, trying to make a good impression—or any combination of these and other factors. Practice witnessing your thoughts, observing your date; and waiting until you have more information before you kick him to the curb or decide he is the one!

- Practice a mantra. If you focus on something, it will manifest in your life. The more you repeat negative thoughts to yourself, the more these become part of who you see yourself as. This applies to dating as well. If you focus on your poor dating experiences, you are sure to have more. If you focus on your flaws, you are sure to highlight them on a date. If you focus on an arbitrary list of attributes your partner must have, you are sure to only see the ways in which this person does not measure up. What if you focus on a positive statement? You are likely to direct your thinking to maintain a positive outlook. According to mindfulness expert Jerry Braza, PhD, when we practice mantras we reduce overall stress and infuse "our consciousness with the messages that positively influence body, mind, and spirit." Studies have shown that the use of mantras is not only effective in helping to create a more positive outlook, but it can also regulate your heart rate, blood pressure, and respiration, in addition to strengthening the immune system, reducing inflammation, and balancing blood sugar levels. The more personal the mantra, the more effective it is. Need I say more?

- Develop healthy self-esteem and self-compassion. It is impossible to have a healthy relationship with a partner if you do not have a healthy relationship with yourself. Your happiness starts from your center out. No relationship will fill a void in you or make you feel complete if you do not feel that way to begin with. You must have confidence in yourself and your abilities. Learn how to soothe and care for yourself. Learn to enjoy spending time with yourself—and get to know who you are and what you have to offer someone else. Treat yourself with kindness and understanding. Accept that you are human, make mistakes, and have flaws like everyone else. This work is essential if you hope to have a long-lasting and healthy relationship with anyone.

Your journey to find companionship, intimacy, pleasure, and connection does not have to be an arduous one. You can find pleasure in the process and learn more about yourself and your needs along the way. Every experience is worthwhile—whether it leads to a committed relationship or not. It is when you let go of your need for things to go a certain way that you make room for things to happen organically. When things happen organically, you will see that your opportunities for a genuine connection are plentiful.

Now you know how to date mindfully. Seeking a soulmate no longer has to send you into a state of panic, resistance, or depression—because you have the tools to navigate the dating world and handle anything that comes your way. Now go out there with fresh eyes and curiosity, and take advantage of all of the possibilities available to you. You deserve love, happiness, and fun. So go get it already!

RELATED RESOURCES

Some of these books are enlightening, some just fun and thought-provoking, but they all have been influential over the years and have helped to shape what I believe in when it comes to finding a partner.

Bass, Ellen. *The Courage to Heal: A Guide for Women Survivors of Childhood Sexual Abuse*, fourth edition. New York: HarperCollins, 2008.

Beck, Aaron T. *Love Is Never Enough: How Couples Can Overcome Misunderstandings, Resolve Conflicts, and Solve Relationship Problems Through Cognitive Therapy*. New York: Harper & Row, 1988.

Beck, Judith, and Aaron T. Beck. *Cognitive Behavioral Therapy: Basics and Beyond*, second edition. New York: The Guildford Press, 2011.

Behrendt, Greg, and Liz Tuccillo. *He's Just Not That Into You: The No-Excuse Truth to Understanding Guys*. New York: Gallery Books, 2009.

Braza, Jerry, and Thich Nhat Hanh. *The Seeds of Love*. North Clarendon, VT: Tuttle, 2011.

Chapman, Gary. *The 5 Love Languages: The Secret to Love That Lasts.* Chicago: Northfield Publishing, 2015.

Fein, Ellen. *All The Rules: Time-Tested Secrets for Capturing the Heart of Mr. Right.* New York: Grand Central Publishing, 2007.

Hanson, Rick, and Richard Mendius. *Buddha's Brain: The Practical Neuroscience of Happiness, Love, and Wisdom.* Oakland, CA: New Harbinger Publications, 2009.

Harvey, Steve, and Denene Millner. *Act Like a Lady, Think Like a Man: What Men Really Think about Love, Relatioships, Intimacy, and Commitment.* New York: Amistad. 2014.

Kabat-Zinn, Jon. *Full Catastrophe Living: Using the Wisdom of Your Body and Mind to Face Stress, Pain, and Illness.* New York, NY: Dell, 1991.

Morin, Jack. *The Erotic Mind: Unlocking the Inner Sources of Passion and Fulfillment. New York: Harper Perennial, 1996.*

Neff, Kristin D. Self-Compassion: The Proven Power of Being Kind to Yourself. New York: William Morrow, 2011.

NurrieStearns, Mary, and Rick NurrieStearns. *Yoga for Anxiety: Meditations and Practices for Calming the Body and Mind.* Oakland, CA: New Harbinger Publications, 2010.

Perel, Esther. *Mating in Captivity: Unlocking Erotic Intelligence.* New York: HarperCollins, 2007.

Singer, Helen Kaplan, and Melvin Horwith. *The Evaluation of Sexual Disorders: Psychological and Medical Aspects.* New York: Brunner/Mazel, 1983.

Steele, David. *Conscious Dating: Finding the Love of Your Life in Today's World.* Campbell, CA: RCN Press, 2006.

Thich Nhat Hanh. *How to Love*. Berkeley, CA: Parallax Press, 2015.

Young, Jeffrey E., PhD, and Janet S. Klosko, PhD. *Reinventing Your Life: The Breakthrough Program to End Negative Behavior and Feel Great Again*. New York: Plume, 1994.

ACKNOWLEDGMENTS

Please bear with me as I take my moment to show love to all of those who have shown love to me.

My mom has been an inspiration my entire life. Everything I do has a little bit of her in it. Her creativity permeated every aspect of what she did, showing me how to be a true renaissance woman. She provided me with love, stability, fun, and encouragement growing up, which have given me the best foundation. Thanks, Mom!

My father showed me that you can do what you love, be dedicated to it, and be very successful at it. His belief in my abilities and support has given me the confidence to say "Yes" even when my anxiety was shouting "NO!" I am grateful for his presence in my life. My stepmom and my in-laws have shown me that blood is not what bonds you. It is the love, support, encouragement, and genuine admiration you share that truly connects you. I am lucky to have you all.

I have to shout out my sibs: Billy, Jamal, Britney, and Nikki, I love you all. My baby bro Jamal still looks at me with those little brother eyes. He makes me feel invincible and I love him for it. And my baby sister Britney feels more like a best friend, confidante, and "ride or die" chick. I don't know what I would do without you, Birtha!

I give many thanks to my cousin Donald, who helped me without hesitation when I have needed him.

Now, I don't mean to brag but I have some of the best friends a gal can have. Special thanks to Micah Guller who told me to blog because "... who knows what can come out of it?" A book can come out of it, Mickey! A freakin' *book!* The brilliant and beautiful Nikki Hart so generously provided me with support and legal advice as I started this venture with no knowledge about the process. Miriam Milord, Christine Morton, Sequoya Maison Blaque, Tajuana Burch, Carla Corona, Jennifer Chang, Leilani Brooks, Helen Yum, Lisa Hammond, Blanca Andrade, and Shelly Roh are all a stable presence in my life and have made me who I am today. We have been through the trauma of being at Ground Zero during 9/11, gotten married, had babies, grown up together, gotten divorced (some of us still trying to get divorced), been detained by security at the mall, been in car accidents together (sometimes more than one on the same day), lived together, had legal issues, gotten into nasty fights, made up, gotten so drunk we ought to be ashamed of ourselves, vacationed together, hooked up with total strangers, and so much more. You guys are my rock. You truly are family to me!

Professionally, I have been inspired by many. Frances Johnson, LCSW-R; Donald Fleck, LCSW, DCSW; Noah Clyman, LCSW-R, ACT; and Ricky Siegal, PhD, LMHC, CST, CSTS; and Daniel Beck, LICSW, have given me support and provided consultation, supervision, and opportunities, giving me a solid foundation in both mindfulness and CBT. The works of Thich Nhat Hanh, Dr. Aaron Beck, Dr. Judith Beck, Ether Perel, Dr. Rick Hanson, Dr. Kristin Neff, Dr. Jon Kabat-Zinn, David Steele, Mary NurrieStearns, Terrence Real, William Masters, and Virginia Johnson, and many, many more have rounded me out as thinker, helper, and teacher.

And of course, I am constantly inspired by my amazing clients. Due to client confidentiality and respect for their personal lives, I never mention my clients by their real names and they may appear as a composite of several different clients in one, but their contributions to this work cannot be denied. Their resilience, courage, and motivation never cease to amaze me. It is an honor to be chosen to support them along their journeys; they have taught me more than I could have ever taught them. I am grateful for the influence that all these people have had in my work and in my life.

I do not even know how to thank my amazing publishing company, Parallax Press. What an honor it is to be working with so many talented individuals. Thank you for seeing something in me and in the work I do. And thank you for making writing my first book a seamless and enjoyable process.

Finally, this book could not have been possible without the three people who have given me the drive to push myself to the limit and work so hard. On March 3, 2000, I went to the Bowery Bar with a group of friends seeking a soulmate. "Where we met, kismet," some might say. That is when the talented, handsome, witty, compassionate life of the party, Brian Ajjan, danced his way into my heart. We met when we were only twenty-two and have grown into lovers, adults, parents, soulmates, and lifelong partners and best friends together. We have created the life I have always wanted and a marriage I never got a chance to witness growing up. Our trials and tribulations only strengthen our bond, and our successes are a testimonial to it. Your faith in me, and in my ability to write this book, is so very appreciated. I literally could not have done this without your picking up the slack when I was busy and encouraging me when I felt incapable of doing more. I am so proud of the man you have become and the family we have created.

Speaking of the family we have created … our daughter Brooklyn Eugenia Ajjan fills my heart with so much joy. She is only eight years old, but I find myself wanting to be more like her. Her spirit, love, kindness, talent, intelligence, beauty, curiosity, generosity, empathy, and enthusiasm inspire me to be better than I was the day before. She inspires me to make her proud of her Mama. And finally there is our little miracle baby boy. Kingston Matteo Ajjan was conceived while I was writing this book. He is still weeks away from being born (as I write this) and he has already made this little family of ours feel more blessed and more complete than I could have ever imagined. He fueled me when I felt burned out and unsure of which direction this book was headed in. Just like daddy! This book is dedicated to the three of you. I love you all more than words could ever express. Thank you for making my dreams come true!

© Mangue Banzima

CHAMIN AJJAN is a licensed clinical social worker. Since 2004, she has led a successful private practice focused on understanding partnerships and romantic relationships. She has written extensively about mindful dating, and developed a mindful dating model that she uses in her practice. She lives with her husband and children in Brooklyn, New York.

 **PARALLAX PRESS**

Parallax Press is a nonprofit publisher, founded and inspired by
Zen Master Thich Nhat Hanh. We publish books on mindfulness
in daily life and are committed to making these teachings acces-
sible to everyone and preserving them for future generations. We
do this work to alleviate suffering and contribute to a more just
and joyful world.

For a copy of the catalog, please contact:

Parallax Press
P.O. Box 7355
Berkeley, CA 94707
(510) 540-6411
parallax.org